THE PEARL
BUYING GUIDE

Text & Photographs

by

RENEE NEWMAN GG

International Jewelry Publications

Los Angeles

International Jewelry Publications
P.O. Box 13384
Los Angeles, CA 90013-0384 USA

(Inquiries should be accompanied by a self-addressed, stamped envelope).

Printed in the United States of America

10   9   8   7   6   5   4   3   2   1

Library of Congress Cataloging in Publication Data

Newman, Renée.
     The pearl buying guide / text & photographs by
Renée Newman.
          p.   cm.
     Includes bibliographical references and index.
     ISBN 0-929975-17-0
     1. Pearls--Purchasing.   I. Title
TS755.P3N49   1992
639'.412--dc20
                                        92-10017
                                        CIP

Cover photograph by
Renée Newman
The necklace is courtesy of the
Josam Diamond Trading Corporation.
It is made of 9 1/2 to 10mm Akoya pearls, one South
Sea pearl, a 17.52-carat sapphire, 2.69 carats of
diamond baguettes and 6.78 carats round brilliant-cut
diamonds.

Contents

Contents

Contents

Acknowledgements

I would like to express my appreciation to the following people for their contribution to *The Pearl Buying Guide*:

Ernie and Regina Goldberger of the Josam Diamond Trading Corporation. This book could never have been written without the experience and knowledge I gained from working with them. Some of the pearls pictured in this book are or were part of their collection.

Charles Carmona, Pin P. Chen, Louise Harris, Susan B. Johnson, Betty Sue King, Peter Malnekoff, Henri Masliah, Lynn Marie Nakamura, and Charles Ueng. They have made valuable suggestions, corrections, and comments regarding the portions of the book they examined. They are not responsible for any possible errors, nor do they necessarily endorse the material contained in this book.

A & Z Pearls Inc., Adachi America Inc., Albert Cohen Co., Overland Gems, Inc., Shima Pearl Company Inc., and Timeless Gem Designs, all in Los Angeles. Their pearls or clasps have been used for some of the photographs.

Albert Asher South Sea Pearl Co., Cultured Pearl Association of America, Inc., Mikimoto Co. Japan Pearl Exporters' Association, King's Ransom, and Frank Mastoloni & Sons, Inc. Photos or diagrams from them have been reproduced in this book.

Ion Itescu, Carl Addicott, Lisa Bishoff, Maria Johnson, and Dawn King. They have provided technical assistance.

Patricia S. Esparza. She has spent hours carefully editing *The Pearl Buying Guide*. Thanks to her, this book is much easier for consumers to read and understand.

My sincere thanks to all of these contributors for their kindness and help.

Suppliers of Pearls & Accessories for Photographs

Cover photo: Josam Diamond Trading Corporation, Los Angeles, CA.

Color photos

#1 Albert Asher South Sea Pearl Co., New York, NY

#3 King's Ransom, Sausalito, California.

#5 Overland Gems, Inc., Los Angeles, CA

#6 Shima Pearl Co., Inc., Los Angeles, CA

#7 Shima Pearl Co., Inc., Los Angeles, CA

Chapter 3

Figs. 3.1 - 3.4 All from the A & Z Pearl, Inc., Los Angeles, CA

Chapter 9

Fig. 9.2 Albert Asher South Sea Pearl Co., New York, NY

Chapter 10

Fig. 10.1 & fig 10.4 Albert Asher South Sea Pcarl Co., New York, NY

Chapter 11

Fig. 11.5   Shima Pearl Co. Inc., Los Angeles, CA

Chapter 14

Fig. 14.4 & 14.8   Timeless Gem Designs, Los Angeles, CA

Fig. 14.5   A & Z Pearls, Inc., Los Angeles, CA

Fig. 14.6   Frank Mastoloni & Sons, Inc., New York, NY

Fig. 14.7   Shima Pearl Co., Inc., Los Angeles, CA

Chapter 15

Figs. 15.1 - 15.15   A & Z Pearls Inc., Los Angeles, CA

Fig. 15.7 (The pearl shortener) Timeless Gem Designs, Los Angeles, CA

Fig. 15.14   (The mabe pearl enhancer)   Shima Pearl Co., Inc., Los Angeles, CA

1

Why Read a Whole Book Just to Buy Some Pearls?

Annemarie turned on the television. A man was advertising a strand of pearls.

"Folks, feast your eyes on this gorgeous strand of pearls.
So lustrous!
So magnificent!
In the stores, you'd be lucky to find these pearls for $900. Even at a half-price sale they would go for $450. But you won't believe your ears when I tell you my give-away price.
Yes, believe it or not--just $139.
Quantities are limited, so don't delay. Mail in your check today. At this price, jewelers will be ordering these strands by the dozens."

Annemarie had been wanting a strand of pearls and this sounded like a fantastic buy, so she sent away for them. When they arrived, they didn't look as lustrous as she had expected. Two weeks later, she took them to her appraiser. He told her it wouldn't be worth getting a written appraisal for them. At best, they might retail for $150. Then he showed her how their pearl coating was peeling off around the drill holes. Once it all peeled off, she would have nothing but a $5 or $10 shell bead necklace.

Annemarie decided to call the phone number on the sales receipt to see how she could return the pearls and get her money back. An operator came on the line. "The number you have dialed has been disconnected."

Joe's grandmother had passed away and his family was having a backyard estate sale. In her jewelry box, there were a lot of cheap-looking pieces that no one figured were worth much. One lady picked out a pair of pearl earrings and asked what their price was. Since they looked better quality than the rest of the jewelry, Joe told her $20 and the lady handed him a twenty-dollar bill. A month later as Joe was going through his grandmother's papers, he discovered an appraisal for a pair of natural pearl earrings valued at $13,000.

Louise was on a Circle Pacific tour that started in Tahiti and ended in Hong Kong. She was shocked at the high prices in Tahiti. The food was expensive enough, but what amazed her most was that black pearls were being sold for $500 apiece.

When Louise arrived in Hong Kong, she saw that she could get a whole strand of black pearls there for $500. She ended up buying three strands.

After Louise returned home, she commented to a jeweler-friend, Maria, about how expensive the black pearls in Tahiti were compared to Hong Kong. Maria told her it was because the pearls in Tahiti were naturally colored instead of dyed like the ones she'd bought in Hong Kong. Maria added that some naturally-colored black pearls had been sold at auction in the United States for over $30,000 apiece.

Louise wished she had known about black pearls before her stay in Tahiti. She would have paid more attention to them and bought a pendant set with one. It would have been an ideal souvenir, unlike anything sold in her hometown.

Adam was in the Orient attending a convention and he wanted to get his wife a nice souvenir. While browsing in a jewelry store near his hotel, his eyes were drawn to a pearl pendant with a strong pink color. Susie, the owner, told him it was a rare Burmese pearl worth over $10,000. She was selling it, though, for just $900. Adam figured this pendant would be a great investment--plus his wife loved pink--so he bought it.

When he returned home, Adam had the pendant appraised. According to the appraisal, the pearl was a dyed mabe pearl--one which is hollowed out, filled with a paste, then covered with a piece of mother of pearl. The retail value of the pendant--$175.

Suppose Adam had had a book which described mabe pearls and discussed dyeing. It would have helped him realize that the pendant was overpriced and that such a strong pink color was probably the result of dye.

Suppose Louise had had a book which explained how black pearls were valued. It would have helped her understand the difference between the pearls she saw in Tahiti and those in Hong Kong.

Suppose Joe had had a book that described how natural pearls were valued and identified. It would have prevented him from practically giving away his grandmother's pearl earrings.

Suppose Annemarie had had a book that showed the quality differences between cheap and valuable pearls. It would have made her question the quality of the advertised pearls since she'd realize that nobody in the jewelry industry can sell their inventory below cost and stay in business. Armed with that knowledge, she would have rightfully suspected that the $900 retail comparison price was overinflated.

If you glance at the table of contents of *The Pearl Buying Guide*, you'll notice a wide range of subjects relevant to buying pearls. There is no way a brochure could cover these subjects adequately. For example, a leaflet can advise you to pay attention to quality differences such as nacre (pearl coating) thickness. But this is not sufficient. You should also know what an acceptable nacre thickness is and how you can determine it. *The Pearl Buying Guide* has the space to provide you with this information.

Besides understanding how to detect quality differences among pearls, you should know how to choose a knowledgeable salesperson. But how do you spot such an individual? Membership in jewelry organizations, extensive sales experience, and gemological credentials do not necessarily indicate that a person has a good knowledge of pearls. (Gemology-diploma courses tend to focus on diamonds and colored stones rather than pearls.) You should judge jewelry professionals by what they know and by their willingness to share this knowledge with you--in other words, by their candor. There are many people from a variety of backgrounds who are well-qualified to sell and appraise pearls. But to determine who these people are, you have to know something about pearls yourself. A book on judging pearl quality not only helps you select pearl jewelry, it also helps you find a good jeweler and appraiser.

What This Book Is Not

♦ It's not a guide to making a fortune on pearls. Nobody can guarantee that gems will increase in value and that they can be resold for more than their retail cost. However, understanding the value concepts discussed in this book can increase your chances of finding good buys on pearls.

♦ It's not a price guide. Pearl prices vary greatly depending on the dealer, the harvest, the rate of currency exchange, and the location where they are sold. Therefore, price lists can be misleading and quickly outdated. Price examples are given, though, to show pearl pricing relationships.

♦ It's not a ten-minute guide to appraising pearls. There's a lot to learn before being able to accurately determine the value of pearls. That's why a book like this is needed on the subject. *The Pearl Buying Guide* is just an introduction, but it does have enough information to give consumers a good background for understanding price differences.

♦ It's not a scientific treatise on the anatomy of a pearl oyster or the chemical, physical, and optical characteristics of a pearl. The material in this book, however, is based on technical research. The appendix lists the properties of pearls; and the chapters on identifying imitation, cultured, and natural pearls refer to these properties. Technical terms needed for buying, grading, or identifying pearls are explained in everyday language.

♦ It's not a discussion about pearl farming or the historical importance of pearls throughout the world. Good books about these subjects have already been written and are included in the bibliography.

♦ It's not a substitute for examining actual pearls. Photographs do not accurately reproduce color, nor do they show the three-dimensional nature of gems very well. Concepts such as luster, orient, and over-tone color are best understood when looking at real pearls.

What This Book Is

♦ A guide to judging the quality and value of the various types of pearls.

♦ An aid to avoiding fraud, with tips on detecting imitation, treated, and assembled pearls.

♦ A handy reference on pearls for laypeople and professionals.

♦ A collection of practical tips on choosing and caring for pearl jewelry.

♦ A challenge to view pearls through the eyes of gemologists and pearl dealers.

How to Use This Book

The Pearl Buying Guide is not meant to be read like a science fiction thriller or a romance novel. Some laypeople may find this book overwhelming at first. It might be advisable for them to start by looking at the pictures and by reading Chapter 2 (Curious Facts about Pearls), Chapter 17 (Finding a Good Buy), and the Table of Contents. Then they should learn the basic terminology in Chapter 3 and continue slowly, perhaps a chapter at a time.

Skip over any sections that don't interest you or that are too difficult. This book has far more information than the average person will care to learn. That's because it's also designed to be a reference. When questions arise about pearls, you can avoid lengthy research by having the answers right at your fingertips.

To get the most out of *The Pearl Buying Guide*, you should try to actively use what you learn. Buy or borrow a loupe (jeweler's magnifying glass) and start examining any pearls you might have at home both with and without the loupe. This will help you learn to distinguish real pearls from imitations and detect quality differences. Take the quizzes that you'll find at the end of many of the chapters. Look around in jewelry stores and ask the professionals there to show you different qualities and types of pearls. If you have pearl appraisals, study them carefully. If there is something you don't understand, ask for an explanation.

Shopping for pearls should not be a chore. It should be fun. There is no fun, though, in worrying about being deceived or in buying pearls that turn out to be a poor choice. Use this book to gain the knowledge, confidence, and independence needed to select the pearls that are best for you. Buying gems represents a significant investment of time and money. Let *The Pearl Buying Guide* help make this investment a pleasurable and rewarding experience.

2

Curious Facts About Pearls

An Apology from the Pearl Family.

We pearls want to express our remorse for the suffering we have brought on to pearl oysters and mussels around the world. Unfortunately, many are not around to receive our long overdue apology.

Consider the pearl oysters in Venezuela and Panama, for example. Five-hundred years ago, these oysters were abundant and had a fairly tranquil life in this area. Then Christopher Columbus and Vasco de Balboa arrived and discovered pearls. Until the development of the gold and silver mines in Mexico and Peru, we pearls were the New World's biggest export. In fact, the value of pearls exceeded that of all other exports combined; and in Spain, the Americas became known as "The Lands that Pearls Come From." One of the most famous members of our pearl family, La Peregrina ("The Incomparable"), was found in the Americas. A pear-shaped pearl about the size of a pigeon's egg, La Peregrina is particularly noted for its beauty.

Among its owners have been Philip II of Spain, Mary Tudor of England, Napoleon III, and Elizabeth Taylor. According to one story, the slave diver that found it was rewarded with his freedom and his master with a plot of land and a position as mayor.

Nowadays the number of oysters producing pearls around Venezuela and Panama is insignificant. One reminder of what an important source of pearls this area once was is the name of an island off the Venezuelan coast, the Isle of Margarita. "Margarita" means pearls. Incidently, if your name is Margaret, Peggy, Marjorie, Margot, Maggie, Gretchen, Gretel, or Rita, it also means "pearl," which in turn signifies purity, innocence, humility, and sweetness.

The overfishing of oysters has not been limited to areas around South and Central America. Pearl oysters and mussels in parts of Europe, North America, and East and West Asia have also either disappeared or been drastically reduced in number.

Besides feeling guilty about the disappearance of so many oysters and mussels, we pearls regret the discomfort we cause to them when they are alive. It might be easier for you to understand what we mean by discomfort if we explained how we originate.

We pearls owe our existence mostly to certain types of saltwater oysters and freshwater mussels. If we are **natural,** then we are usually formed as the mollusk secretes layers of a protective, pearly substance called **nacre** (pronounced NAY-ker) around an irritant. This irritant, which is our **nucleus,** accidentally enters the mollusk and can be a minute snail, worm, fish or crab, or a particle of shell, clay or mud. Experimentation and pearl slicing, however, have led some pearl researchers to believe that most natural round pearls are caused by the accidental entry of a parasitic worm into a mollusk. There aren't many natural pearls produced anymore for them to study. The pearls that are sold today are usually cultured.

If we are **cultured,** then the irritant is intentionally introduced by man. In the case of most freshwater pearls, pieces of mantle (a membranous tissue that secretes nacre and lines the inner shell surface of mollusks) are inserted into a mussel or oyster. Saltwater cultured pearls, however, usually originate from the insertion of a shell bead nucleus along with a bit of oyster mantle tissue into an oyster. In both cases, the shape and size of the resulting pearls depends to a large degree on the shape and size of the implanted irritant.

Sometimes people are surprised to discover how small oysters are for the pearls they host. Japanese pearl oysters grow to only about 10 centimeters (4") in diameter. Imagine what it would be like if you had to carry around a baseball inside of you. This will help you understand why we feel bad about oysters having to put up with us. Besides being a source of irritation, we also lead to their premature death. Many cultured pearl oysters die when a nucleus is inserted or when pearls are later removed.

As we pearls take this occasion to apologize for the miserable fate that we have brought on to the pearl oysters and mussels of this world, we would also like to express our gratitude for their hospitality. Were it not for the oyster and mussel, we pearls would not have the chance to exist.

The Pearl Oysters' Response

We oysters don't harbor any grudges against pearls. They have made our lives worthwhile. Pearls are not responsible for killing off pearl mollusks. Man is. Consider the mussels in Lake Biwa, Japan. They used to be plentiful. Now, due to pollution, the few that are left are struggling to survive.

Consider too the oysters in the Persian gulf. They used to be renowned for producing the world's finest natural pearls. Overfishing plus the discovery of oil and industrialization of the gulf have disrupted the oyster beds there.

As for the pearls' concern about irritating us or causing us pain, their worries are exaggerated. Our nervous system is very simple. Consequently, we don't have the same sense of feeling that humans do.

The fame and prestige that pearls have brought to us oysters has more than made up for the minor discomfort it has caused. Maybe you find it hard to understand how something as plain as a pearl could elevate our status. Some background information on it might help explain why.

The pearl is the oldest known gem, and for centuries it was considered the most valuable. To the ancients, pearls were a symbol of the moon and had magical powers which could bring prosperity and long life.

Throughout history, pearls have been considered divine gifts especially suited for royalty. Women who wanted to gain the favor of a king would offer him pearls. In Persia, crowns with double circlets of pearls were the symbol of royal and divine birth. This became a custom elsewhere as well. When Julius Caesar became emperor of the Roman empire, he claimed descent from the gods and was crowned with a pearl diadem.

Pearls, too, have been considered ideal wedding gifts due to their symbolism of purity and innocence. In the Hindu religion, the presentation of an undrilled pearl and its piercing has formed part of the marriage ceremony.

Some cultures, such as the Chinese, have used pearls medically to cure a variety of ailments--indigestion, fever, heart disease. Pearls have also been prescribed as a love potion and tonic for long life. Today, the main component of pearls, calcium carbonate ($CaCO_3$), is used as an antacid and a dietary supplement. Calcium manganese carbonate is an important heart medicine. At the age of 94, Mikimoto, the founder of the cultured pearl industry stated, "I owe my fine health and long life to the two pearls I have swallowed every morning of my life since I was twenty."

Fig. 2.1 Cultured pearl in a freshly opened oyster. Photo courtesty Japan Pearl Exporters' Association.

The unique qualities of the pearl were particularly well described by George Kunz and Charles Stevenson in 1908 in The Book of the Pearl (page 305).

> Unlike other gems, the pearl comes to us perfect and beautiful, direct from the hand of nature. Other precious stones receive careful treatment from the lapidary, and owe much to his art. The pearl, however, owes nothing to man...It is absolutely a gift of nature, on which man cannot improve. We turn from the brilliant, dazzling ornament of diamonds or emeralds to a necklace of pearls with a sense of relief, and the eye rests upon it with quiet, satisfied repose and is delighted with its modest splendor, its soft gleam, borrowed from its home in the depths of the sea. It seems truly to typify steady and abiding affection, which needs no accessory or adornment to make it more attractive. And there is a purity and sweetness about it which makes it especially suitable for the maiden.

Had it not been for the pearl, we oysters would have probably been scorned as lowly, slothful creatures. Instead we're recognized as the creator of an extraordinary gem--one symbolic of all that is pure and beautiful. Therefore we'd like to take this occasion to thank all pearls for the esteem they have brought to our species. We oysters are proud to be their hosts.

3

Pearl Types & Shapes

When you think of a pearl, what's the first shape and color that comes to your mind? Probably round and white. But if you lived in Tahiti, you might initially think of a dark grayish pearl and it wouldn't necessarily be round. If you lived in China, you might first think of a crinkled irregularly shaped pearl. Pearls come in a wide range of shapes, types, and colors; and it is the aim of this chapter to define the various types and to explain the role that shape plays in determining the value of a pearl.

Pearl Types

The difference between natural and cultured pearls was explained in Chapter 2. Technically the term **pearl** should only refer to a natural pearl. Nevertheless, cultured pearls are so common now and natural ones so rare that "pearl" normally refers to a cultured pearl (One exception is in certain Arab countries where cultured pearls tend to be frowned upon. Pearls there are generally considered a special gift from God that should be entirely a product of nature.) In this book, for the sake of brevity, cultured pearls will often be labeled as "pearls." When shopping for pearls, you may come across the term **semi-cultured**. It refers to imitation pearls. Many members of the trade consider it a deceptive term designed to trick buyers into thinking they are getting cultured pearls when they aren't. According to *National Jeweler Magazine* (Nov. 1, 91), some in-flight duty-free magazines have been advertising "semi-cultured" pearls.

Pearls can additionally be classed as saltwater or freshwater. People tend to be most familiar with **saltwater pearls**, which come from oysters in oceans, seas, gulfs, and bays. The best-known example is the Akoya pearl shown in figure 3.1 and discussed below.

Fig. 3.1 Japanese Akoya pearls (cultured saltwater pearls)

Freshwater pearls are found in mussels or oysters in rivers and lakes and tend to be more irregular in shape and more varied in color than pearls found in saltwater oysters (fig. 3.2, & color photos 3, 5 & 6). Chapter 11 provides more information and photos on freshwater pearls.

Pearls are further classified into the categories below:

Oriental Pearls Natural pearls found in oysters of the Persian Gulf or those that look like pearls found there (according to the USA Federal Trade Commission). Some-times this term is used to designate either any natural saltwater pearl or else more specifically, any natural saltwater pearl found in the West Asia Area, e.g. in the Red Sea, the Persian Gulf, or the Gulf of Mannar off the west coast of Sri Lanka.

A more precise definition of "Oriental pearl" is offered by the respected pearl researcher, Koji Wada, in Pearls of the World (page 69)--natural pearls from one kind of sea-water pearl oyster called the wing shell.

Akoya Pearls Saltwater pearls from the Akoya oyster (Pinctada fucata martensii), which are usually cultured. These pearls are typically roundish and more or less white (fig. 3.1). The chapters on pearl quality in this book focus on Akoya pearls.

Even though they are often called Japanese pearls, they can also be found in oysters outside Japan. Shohei Shirai in his book *Pearls* (pg. 9 & 10) points out that Japanese Akoya oysters also inhabit the tropical seas. His research and on-site surveys have shown that Korea, China, Hong Kong, and Sri Lanka are already culturing pearls using the Akoya oyster. However, most Akoya pearls found in jewelry stores are cultured in Japan.

South Sea Pearls

As a general term, it can signify any saltwater pearl found in the area extending from Burma down to Australia and across to French Polynesia. It's often used more specifically to refer to large white pearls cultured in the Pinctada maxima oyster--a large oyster found in the South Seas, which is also called the silver-lip or gold-lip oyster depending on the color of its shell lip (color photo #1).

South Sea pearls tend to range from 9mm to 16mm, whereas Akoya pearls usually range from 2mm to 9mm. A more detailed discussion of South Sea pearls is found in Chapter 9.

Biwa Pearls

Freshwater pearls cultivated in Lake Biwa, Japan's largest lake (fig. 3.2). Sometimes other freshwater cultured pearls are called Biwas in order to impress buyers. Lake Biwa was one of the first freshwater culturing sites and it has been noted for its high quality pearls. Due to pollution, production has come to a standstill.

Fig. 3.2 Left: Chinese freshwater pearl, right: Biwa pearl (Japanese freshwater pearl)

Black Pearls

Dark-colored pearls of natural color (not dyed) from the black-lip (Pinctada margaritifera) oyster (color photo #8). Some people use the term "black pearl" to refer to any dark colored pearl. Chapter 10 provides more information about them.

Blue Pearls

Dark-colored pearls found in oysters such as the Akoya or silver-lip oysters. The color is due to foreign contaminants in the nacre or between the nacre and shell bead nucleus unlike black pearls whose color is an inherent characteristic of the of the pearl nacre. (Hisada and Komatsu, *Pearls of the World*, p.88 and Robert Webster, *Gems*, p. 506).

Mother of Pearl

The smooth, hard pearly lining on the interior of a mollusk shell, which is used to make decorative objects, buttons, and beads. Cultured pearls are a lot more expensive than mother-of-pearl beads even though pearl nacre and mother of pearl are composed of basically the same pearly substance ($CaCO_3$ and a little water and conchiolin, a binding agent). Mother of pearl, however, generally has a slightly higher percentage of water and conchiolin than pearl nacre.

Half Pearls

"Whole pearls that have been ground or sawed on one side, usually to remove blemishes" (as defined in *The GIA Jeweler's Manual*). If about 3/4 of the pearl remains, it's called a **three-quarter pearl**.

The term "half pearl" is also used to refer to blister pearls, especially outside the United States.

Blister Pearls

Natural or cultured pearls that grow attached to the inner surface of the oyster or mussel shell. When cut from the shell, one side is left flat with no pearly coating. (Some people apply the term "blister" only to natural pearls of this type.)

Cultured blister pearls are not new. As far back as the 13th century, the Chinese were placing small lead images of the sitting Buddha inside freshwater mussels against their shells. The resulting pearly buddhas were either removed and sold as good-luck charms or else left attached to the shell and used as an ornamental curiosity.

Mabe Pearls

Assembled cultured blister pearls (fig 3.3) (pronounced MAH-bay). The blister pearl is cultured by gluing against the inside of the shell a half-bead nucleus (often of plastic or soapstone). After the mollusk has secreted nacre over the bead, the blister pearl is cut from the shell; and the bead is removed so the pearl can be cleaned to prevent deterioration. The remaining hole is filled with a paste or wax (and sometimes also a bead) and then covered with a mother-of-pearl backing.

Fig. 3.3 Mabe pearls

It can be hard to distinguish between mabe, blister, or half pearls when they are mounted in jewelry. As a consequence, these three terms often end up being used interchangeably.

Despite all the work involved in assembling mabe pearls, they are relatively inexpensive for their large size. This is partly because several can be grown in one oyster and because they are grown in oysters that have rejected a whole nucleus or that are judged unsuitable for producing whole pearls. Also, any type of half pearl will cost far less than if it were whole, no matter what type of oyster it is grown in.

Most large mabe assembled pearls come from the silver-lip or black-lip oysters, but technically the term "**mabe**" should only refer to pearls cultivated in mabe oysters (Pteria penguin, penguin wing). The true **mabe-oyster pearls** are known for having a better luster, color, and iridescence than pearls cultured in other oysters and are, consequently, more valuable (color photo #7). Most of those harvested are 1/2 or 3/4 blister pearls. If a salesperson claims that the jewelry you are buying is made with a mabe-oyster pearl, have him or her write this on the receipt. It's helpful for insurance and appraisal purposes. Information on the culturing of mabe oysters can be found in a write-up by Morimitsu Muramatsu in *Pearls of the World* (pp. 79 to 86).

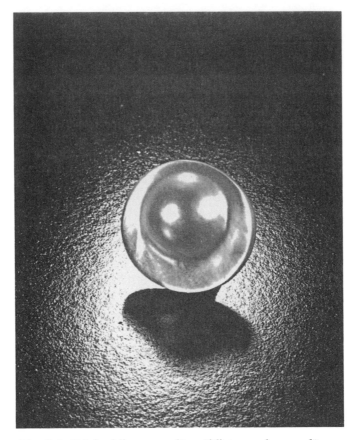

Fig. 3.4 "Mabe blister pearl" or "blister mabe pearl"

"Mabe Blister Pearls"   An informal term used by some dealers to designate mabe pearls with a nacre rim, making them resemble a fried egg (fig. 3.4). The term "blister mabe" is also used. Technically, though, all assembled mabe pearls originate as blister pearls.

Seed Pearls   Small, natural pearls which measure about two millimeters or less. They usually weigh less than 0.06 carat.

Dust Pearls   Tiny pearls that weigh less than 0.01 carat and that are too small to be useful for jewelry.

Keshi   Pearls that grow accidentally in the soft tissue or the adductor muscle of cultured pearl-bearing mollusks. "Keshi" is the term for poppy seed in Japanese. It originated from the minute pearls that were spontaneously formed when a much larger pearl with a bead nucleus was cultured in the Akoya oyster. To the Japanese, these tiny pearls without nuclei resembled poppy seeds, hence the name. After the larger Akoya cultured pearls are removed from the shell, the keshis are collected. Then they are usually exported to countries where the labor costs of drilling and stringing them is low. A high percentage of keshi pearls are ground up and used for medicinal purposes in places such as China, India, and Hong Kong.

Today the term "keshi" also refers to the bigger pearls without nuclei that are spontaneously formed in South Sea and freshwater cultured pearls. These can exceed 10mm in width and 10mm in length so they are set in rings, pendants, brooches and earrings and are sometimes made into strands. Fine keshi pearls are noted for their high luster and iridescence and unique shapes. Compared to fine round pearls, their prices are very reasonable.

There is a lot of debate in the trade as to whether keshi pearls should be considered natural pearls. Like natural pearls, they grow accidentally, but they form in oysters that are cultivated by man. The question of whether keshi can properly be called natural has not yet been resolved. However, many Arabs have already made up their mind. They are among the largest buyers of keshi and prefer to regard them as natural.

Mikimoto pearls Pearls produced and marketed by the Mikimoto Co. Even though Mikimoto pearls come in a range of qualities, they are known for having a higher luster and fewer flaws than the average Akoya pearl. The Mikimoto Co. estimates that only a small fraction of the pearls produced meet the requirements for carrying their trademark clasp. Other companies, too, produce and market pearls of the same high quality standards as those of the Mikimoto Co. Only the name is different.

Consumers should be aware that the Mikimoto name has been misrepresented in some jewelry stores and some discount places. Therefore, **don't assume that pearls with a label saying "Mikimoto" are Mikimoto pearls. Look at the clasp.** Only those pearls which have an 18-karat-gold Mikimoto signature clasp are true Mikimoto pearls. Either a pearl or a diamond will be in the center of it. Also, when you buy Mikimoto pearls, ask the jeweler for the Mikimoto certificate of authenticity that should come with them.

The founder of Mikimoto Pearls, Kokichi Mikimoto, was a pearl farmer, researcher, and merchant who brought respectability to the cultured pearl. In essence, he is the founder of the cultured pearl industry. He is also credited with inventing most of the techniques of oyster farming used today. Using some of Mikimoto's methods,

Tatsuhei Mise and Tokichi Nishikawa in 1907, each became the first to invent techniques for culturing round pearls.

In the early 1900's when round cultured pearls were first sold to the public, they were considered by some as fraudulent imitations. In 1921, suits were filed in London and Paris to prevent Mikimoto from selling his cultured pearls. Mikimoto responded by filing suit to stop people from selling imitation pearls as cultured, and he persuaded the French Customs Bureau to charge the same import duty on both natural and cultured pearls. Cultured pearls had previously been classed as costume jewelry. Mikimoto also spent a great deal of time worldwide educating the jewelry trade and the general public about cultured pearls. As a result, cultured pearls became a desireable commodity and are no longer considered imitations. And Mikimoto, son of a poor noodle vendor, came to be known as "The Pearl King."

Pearls Produced by Snails

A hundred years ago, pearls were often broadly defined as any gem grown by a shell animal to protect itself from an irritant. Today, gem laboratories such as the GIA Gem Trade Lab are more strict and would not classify the conch "pearl," for example, as a true pearl. This is because it lacks layers of nacre. This book is about pearls found in oysters and mussels. However, for the sake of interest, it briefly describes the following snail "pearls" because they are sold as pearls.

Abalone "pearls"   Found in abalone off the coast of New Zealand, California, Mexico, Japan, and Korea, these "pearls" are known for their colorful, almost opal-like appearance. They may be any combination of green, blue, pink, or yellow and usually have an irregular shape, sometimes resembling a tooth or a cone. The finest-quality abalone "pearls" are collectors items and may sell for between $5,000 and $15,000.

The September 1991 issue of *Modern Jeweler* reported that about 20,000 saleable cultured abalone "pearls" had been harvested in Korea in 1990. These "pearls" sold in Singapore for as much as $385 per "pearl."

Conch "pearls"   Also called "pink pearls"--though many are brownish or white--they are found in the great Conch, a large marine snail found throughout the Caribbean. They may have distinctive flame-like surface markings and the best ones tend to be symmetrical in shape and often oblong. Fine conch "pearls" may cost between $1000 and $10,000 and tend to be most appreciated by Europeans and Arabs.

1. South Sea pearl necklace and earrings. Photo courtesy Albert Asher South Sea Pearl Co.

2. Left--cream-color pearls with various overtones, center--white imitation pearls, right--pink pearls with pink and green over-tones.

3. Biwa, Chinese freshwater, mabe and black pearls along with Madagascar tourmaline. Photo courtesy King's Ransom.

4. Pink dye in pearl drill hole

5. Chinese freshwater pearls

6. Japanese freshwater pearl (Biwa)

7. Blister pearl from the mabe oyster. Note the iridescence

8. Natural-color black pearl

Fig. 3.5 Osmena or nautilus "pearl"

Osmena "Pearls   "White or Gray "pearls" which, according to sellers, are grown in the chambered nautilus snail from the Philippines (fig. 3.5). Like mabes, these "pearls" are filled with a kind of paste and then covered with a backing. Occasionally, they can be found on sale at gem shows for prices as low as $5 and $10. They may be used as pendants or earrings. Commercially, osmena "pearls" (also called nautilus "pearls") are not important.

Judging shape

Shape plays a major role in determining the price of pearls. Throughout history, round has generally been considered the most valuable shape for a pearl. Perhaps this was because pearls were considered a symbol of the moon. Nevertheless, the most famous and valuable pearls are often not round. That's because factors such as size, luster, and origin are also important.

Pearls can be divided into four basic shape categories:

♦ **Round**   (fig 3.6)

♦ **Off-Round**   Slightly flattened or ovalish (fig. 3.7)

33

♦ **Semi-Baroque**   Obviously not round (fig. 3.8). Pear, drop, egg, and button shapes are examples.

♦ **Baroque**   Very distorted and irregular in shape (fig. 3.9). Often the surface is very uneven. They occasionally resemble familiar objects such as teeth, cacti, tadpoles, mushrooms, or snails.

Fig. 3.6 Round

Fig. 3.7 Off-round

Fig. 3.8 Semi-baroque

Fig. 3.9 Baroque

Sometimes additional categories are added for evaluating shape. For example, the sub-categories of "mostly round" and "slightly off-round" are used along with the four basic ones above in the pearl grading system of the GIA (Gemological Institute of America).

Akoya pearl prices are generally based on round pearls. When the pearls deviate from the round shape, they are discounted. Adachi America, a pearl company that has developed a "master set" pearl grading program, has the following discount schedule for their Akoya pearls:

Semi-round   10 to 25% less than round
Semi-baroque   25 to 55% less than round
Baroque   55 to 80% less than round

Midwest Gem Lab, who also offers a master-strand pearl grading system, has another discount schedule, which is based on a survey of some Akoya pearl dealers:

Off-round	0 to 10% less than round
Semi-baroque	10 to 30% less than round
Baroque	70 to 80% less than round*

           * This is only a general indication. For more exact pricing of baroques, quotes should be obtained from dealers.

The following conclusions can be drawn when comparing these two discount schedules:

♦ Shape can have a significant effect on the price of pearls.
♦ Pearl pricing can vary from one dealer to another.
♦ The upper and lower boundaries of each shape category need to be clearly defined and illustrated (so far this has not been done in the trade). It appears, for example, that the dealers Midwest Gem Lab surveyed had a fairly restricted interpretation of "baroque." Perhaps these dealers and Adachi price baroques alike, but to know this, we need to see what range of shapes each dealer classifies as baroque.

When judging pearls for shape, take into consideration the type of pearl you are looking at. For example, expensive natural pearls are typically baroque, whereas cheap cultured pearls with thin nacre (pearl coating) are generally round. That's because natural pearls don't contain a round nucleus bead, and cultured pearl beads that are hardly coated with nacre don't have much of a chance to grow irregular. The typical shapes of five pearl types are described below to help you know what degree of roundness to expect of pearls. They are listed from the most commonly round to the most commonly baroque.

Akoya pearls with thin nacre	Often round
Akoya pearls with thick nacre	Frequently off-round, but round ones are available too. Baroque Akoya pearl strands are considered low quality.
South Sea cultured	Rarely perfectly round. The larger the pearl, the more it will tend to deviate from round. Baroques are often regarded as a good alternative to the more expensive symmetrical shapes when ones budget is limited.
Natural saltwater	Usually baroque or semi-baroque. Round ones are extremely rare.
Freshwater, cultured & natural	Usually baroque, especially if they are natural. Baroque freshwater pearls are considered desirable. Cultured off-round freshwater pearls are available. They are normally more affordable than saltwater pearls of similar quality and size.

Another grading factor to consider when judging off-round and especially semi-baroque pearls is their **degree of symmetry** (perfectly round pearls are always symmetrical and baroque pearls are by definition unsymmetrical). If for example, you are buying a teardrop pearl pendant for someone special, one with two equal sides would probably be the most desireable. Lopsided pearls can be interesting but they are considered less valuable than those which are symmetrical.

Even though dealers agree round is the most expensive shape, there is no standardized system for determining how shape affects pearl prices. As previously mentioned, the way pearls are discounted for shape variation can differ from one dealer to another. Do not let this lack of standardization lead you to ignore pearl shape as a value factor. Consider it important, and keep in mind when judging pearl prices that it's best to compare pearls of the same shape as well as the same size, color, type, and luster.

Quiz (Chapters 2 and 3)

Select the correct answer.

1. A mother-of-pearl bead is:

a. as valuable as a pearl
b. less valuable than a pearl
c. more valuable than a pearl
d. another name for a pearl

2. Which of the following types of pearls is most likely to be round?

a. A cultured South Sea pearl
b. A natural South Sea pearl
c. An Akoya pearl with very thin nacre
d. An Akoya pearl with very thick nacre

3. Mikimoto pearls:

a. come from a special kind of oyster trademarked by the Mikimoto company.
b. have more flaws than most pearls.
c. come in a range of qualities.
d. are natural pearls.

4. Baroque pearls:

a. originate from Europe.
b. have irregular shapes.
c. are freshwater pearls.
d. are those set in ornate mountings.

5. Mabe assembled pearls may come from:

a. The mabe oyster
b. The white South Sea pearl (silver-lip) oyster
c. The black pearl (black-lip) oyster
d. All of the above

6. Semi-cultured pearls:

a. are imitation pearls.
b. are half natural and half cultured.
c. have a cultivation period which is half as long as that of a cultured pearl.
d. grow in oysters which are bred in a laboratory.

7. High-quality keshi pearls are noted for their:

a. high luster
b. unique shapes
c. iridescence
d. all of the above

8. A salesperson shows you a pearl necklace which he says is Mikimoto promotional-quality. It does not have an 18-karat gold Mikimoto clasp. Which of the following is true?

a. The pearls are probably of high quality.
b. The salesperson is misrepresenting the pearls and misusing the Mikimoto name.
c. The Mikimoto company forgot to put their trademark clasp on the necklace.

True or false?

9. Cultured pearls are imitation pearls grown by man in the Akoya oyster.

10. A pearl must be round to be valuable.

11. Freshwater pearls are those which are cultivated in non-polluted waters.

12. Valuable natural pearls have been found in North, South, and Central America.

13. Cultured round pearls were first produced and marketed in the early 1900's
.

14. Natural pearls are produced by implanting shell beads in oysters which breed naturally.

15. Nacre is the pearly substance secreted around an irritant by an oyster or mussel.

16. When judging prices consumers should try to compare pearls of the same shape and type.

Answers:

1. b

2. c

3. c

4. b

5. d

6. a

7   d

8. b

9. F   They are not imitation pearls.

10. F

11. F

12. T

13. T

14. F

15. T

16. T

4

Judging Luster & Nacre Thickness

"PEARLS--HALF OFF!"

Does this indicate a bargain? Who knows? It might even mean "Nacre--Half Off." No matter what their price, pearls aren't much of a bargain if they're dull-looking or their nacre (pearl coating, pronounced NAY-ker) peels away.

Normally thin nacre means low luster, but there are thin-nacre pearls with good luster and thick-nacre pearls with low luster. Consequently, it's best to treat luster and nacre thickness as two separate value factors.

What is Pearl Luster?

The noted gemologist, Robert Webster, defines **luster** as the surface brilliancy of a gemstone, which depends on the quality and quantity of the reflected light. When the term "luster" is applied to pearls, it tends to have a broader meaning. It also refers to the light reflected off the internal layers of nacre. In other words, a lustrous pearl has more than just a shiny, reflective surface. It also has a glow from within.

Compare, for example, the pearl to a highly polished gold bead. The gold bead will usually have sharper surface reflections than the pearl, but that doesn't mean it's more lustrous. In fact, it's more conventional to describe gold as shiny, bright, or metallic. Brilliant pearls, on the other hand, are more frequently termed lustrous.

Pearls with a very high luster will generally show the following characteristics when viewed under a bare light with the naked eye.

♦ Strong light reflections
♦ Sharp light reflections
♦ A good contrast between the bright and darker areas of the pearl

(Many pearl experts would also list iridescence as a characteristic because lustrous pearls not only reflect light, they break it up into different colors. On round pearls the iridescence tends to be very subtle, and a pinkish tone may result. On high luster baroque pearls, you may see flashes of rainbow colors. Since iridescence is a color phenomenon, this book has it listed as a quality factor in the chapter on color.)

The evaluation of luster will be discussed in a later section. But first, it's helpful to know why pearls vary in luster.

What Determines Luster?

The luster of a pearl depends on the quality of the nacre--it's transparency, smoothness and overall thickness as well as the thickness of each of the microscopic layers of nacre. Under an electron microscope, the nacre crystals of lustrous pearls have a strong hexagonal form and are regularly distributed, whereas the crystals forming the nacre of lifeless pearls lack a clear outline, are thinly scattered, or are irregularly deposited (from *The Retail Jeweller's Guide*, p 90, by Kenneth Blakemore).

The quality of the nacre, and in turn the luster, is affected by a variety of factors such as:

♦ Cultivation techniques used
♦ Cultivation place
♦ Health of mother oyster
♦ Length of time pearl is in oyster
♦ Time of year when pearl is harvested
♦ Pollution
♦ Abnormally wide variations in temperature
♦ Type of oyster used. For example, the mabe oyster (found mainly in the tropical seas of Southeast Asia) can produce a pearl with a higher luster than those of the South Seas silver-lip oyster. The Akoya oyster is also noted for its capacity to produce pearls of high luster.

High luster is not merely the result of leaving a pearl in an Akoya oyster for an adequate length of time. As one can infer from the above list, cultivating a lustrous pearl is a complex process, and it involves skill and chance.

Judging Luster

Suppose we could line up all the pearls in the world according to the quality of their luster. We would notice that a very low percentage of the pearls would be at the end of the line with the best luster. We would also notice that the pearls would very gradually change in luster as we went down the line. In other words, there would be no distinct luster categories.

We could, however, divide the line of pearls into any number of equal ranges (categories) of luster. Then we could assign a luster name to each category such as **very high**, **high**, **medium**, **low and very low**. Luster categories like this are found in the GIA (Gemological Institute of America) pearl grading system. Pearl dealers have their own in-house grading systems, which often combine various value factors. However, many dealers might feel that the terms **"gem quality"** or **"AAAA"** should only be applied to pearls having an exceptionally high luster. Don't assume, though, that a pearl strand labeled "AAAA" or "Gem" is necessarily top quality. It's a common practice to misuse grades by applying high ones to lower quality goods.

Very high luster pearls have sharp, intense, almost mirror-like light reflections, and there is a high contrast between their bright and dark areas. Such pearls are not always easy to find. In fact, you may be lucky to find a store in your area that has them in stock. Expect to pay premium prices for these pearls. For example, strands of very-high-luster, round, white pearls over 6 1/2 mm won't be priced in the hundreds of dollars. They will be in the thousands of dollars. The actual cost of the strands will be determined by a variety of factors.

Very low luster pearls are easy to spot. They look very milky or chalky, and seem more like a white bead than a pearl. This is due to the low contrast between the light and dark areas of the pearls. Some jewelers won't stock this type of pearl, but others will. This is also the type of pearl a mail order place might be tempted to sell. The customer doesn't see what he's getting. He only sees the super low price listed in the catalogue.

Fig. 4.1 Top strand: high luster, middle strand: medium luster, bottom strand: low and very low luster. Note how the dark areas become lighter as the luster decreases.

Fig. 4.2 Shiny white plastic beads and pearl strand with a fluorescent desk lamp lighting them from 1 yard (1 meter) away. Even though the surface reflection is sharper on the beads, the pearls are more lustrous because of their stronger glow. Note the low luster of the center pearl and how little contrast there is between its darker and lighter areas.

Fig. 4.3 Same beads and pearls with same light 10 inches away. The light reflection is larger than figure 4.2, which can make it appear to have a stronger glow.

Fig. 3.4 Same beads and pearls with same light covered with a white cloth (diffused lighting). The light is about 14 inches from the pearls. Note the lower luster appearance and the lower contrast between the darker and lighter areas of the beads and pearls.

The majority of the pearls sold in stores probably fall in the low and medium luster ranges. Many fine-quality jewelry stores also stock high-luster pearls. The best way to learn to recognize high-, medium-, and low-luster pearls is to look at strands representing these luster ranges. Some jewelers may show you short master strands illustrating these or similar categories, but they may use different category names such as "bright," "commercial," "AAA," etc. Top-quality pearl salespeople are eager to help you see luster differences so you'll know what you are getting for your money. They don't want their prices unfairly compared to stores offering low-quality "bargain" pearls.

As you shop for pearls and examine them for luster, keep in mind that the pearl industry has not yet adopted a standardized system for grading pearls. What one jeweler considers low luster another might call high. Therefore, **don't rely just on word descriptions of pearls.** What your eyes see is what counts most. Verbal descriptions are merely guides. If you have any strands of pearls at home, it's a good idea to take them along and use them as a basis for comparison. Even pearl dealers rely on comparison strands when buying pearls.

Also keep in mind the following tips when shopping:

♦ Examine the strands on a flat white surface, e.g. a white cloth, board, or paper). Luster is hard to judge when pearls are suspended or on a dark surface.

♦ If possible, examine the pearls directly under a bare light instead of away from the light. This helps bring out their luster. (Lighting is discussed more in detail in the next section).

◆ Look for the brightest and darkest areas of the pearls. Then compare the contrast between the two. The lower the contrast and the milkier the pearl, the lower the luster. This is one of the quickest and easiest ways to spot low and very low luster. Milky-looking pearls are sometimes sold in "high quality" stores. Be aware that their luster is low.

◆ Examine the light reflections on the pearls. Usually, the less sharp and intense they are, the lower the luster. Sometimes, however, a lack of sharpness is due to surface flaws, rather than the overall luster.

◆ Compare the lusters of the individual pearls on the strand. They will almost always vary somewhat in luster. The luster quality of a strand is determined by its overall appearance, not just by one pearl. High-luster strands, however, should not have low- and very-low-luster pearls. If you find a strand you like that happens to have a pearl or two with an obviously lower luster than the rest of the strand, ask the salesperson to have them changed when they are strung with a clasp.

◆ Roll the pearls slightly so you can see their entire surface. The luster not only varies from pearl to pearl. It varies on each pearl.

◆ If possible, lay the pearls alongside other strands and compare the lusters. This is most effective when you already know the relative quality of the comparison strands. Keep in mind that your impression of a strand will be affected by the pearls it is compared to. A strand will look better when viewed next to lower-luster strands than next to those of higher luster.

◆ Try the pearls on and check if you can see the highlighted spots on them from a distance (say 10 feet/3 meters). You'll be able to if the pearls are of good quality.

Sometimes buyers get so involved in examining the shape and blemishes of pearls that they overlook their luster. The Japan Pearl Exporters' Association would consider this a big mistake. According to their booklet *Cultured Pearls*, "The most important value point in pearls of equal size is luster because that is what gives a pearl its beauty."

How Lighting Affects Luster

Gemologists and appraisers normally grade pearls under standardized lighting conditions. When shopping for pearls, you will encounter various lighting situations. You need to understand, therefore, how lighting affects the appearance of pearls in order to avoid being misled.

The main thing to remember is the stronger and more direct the light, the more lustrous the pearls will look. Ask yourself:

◆ Is the lighting diffused? For example, is the light covered with a white shade? Is the light coming through curtains, clouds, or translucent glass? The more diffused the light is, the lower the luster will appear to be. Bare lights or direct sunlight, on the other hand, will bring out the luster of pearls (figs. 4.2 to 4.4).

♦ How intense is the light? In the case of sunlight, is it early morning or midday? Midday sunlight will bring out the luster more. In the case of light bulbs, are they 60 watt or 150 watt? The higher the wattage, the more lustrous your pearls will look.

♦ How close is the light to the pearls? The further the light is from the pearls, the smaller and less intense the reflections become and the less the pearls seem to glow (figs. 4.2 & 4.3).

If it's possible for you to carry or wear comparison strands of pearls, do so. You'll be able to compare known strands with unknown ones under equal lighting conditions, and it will be easier for you to tell the effect of the lighting on both.

Judging Nacre Thickness

If you were to cut a 7-mm Akoya cultured pearl in half, you would see a large core inside. It would be a bead probably cut from an American mussel shell. The outside of the bead would be encircled with a pearly layer of nacre. If the pearl had been left in the oyster for just six months, the layer would be very thin, too thin to be very durable or lustrous.

Before about 1960, Japanese Akoya pearl farmers left the pearls in the oyster for at least two and a half years. Mikimoto left his in for over three years for maximum nacre thickness. Then many farmers dropped the time to one and a half years. Around 1979, pearl harvesting started to be done just after 6-8 months. The result--a lot of inexpensive, low-quality pearls on the market. And they are still out there, being offered at rock-bottom prices. The buyers end up with shell beads and hardly any pearl. Fortunately, better pearls with thicker nacre are also available, but rarely as thick as those cultured before the 1960's. The goal of this section is to help you determine if the nacre thickness of the pearls you look at is acceptable or not.

The GIA, in their pearl grading course, has defined 5 levels of nacre thickness for Akoya cultured pearls. They are:

Very thick	At least 0.5 mm on all the pearls of the strand
Thick	At least 0.5 mm on most pearls of the strand
Medium	0.35 - 0.5 mm on most pearls
Thin	0.25 - 0.35 mm on most pearls
Very thin	0.25 mm or less on most pearls

Pearl dealers don't need to measure the nacre to determine if it's thin or very thin. They know just by looking at the pearls. Some clues are:

♦ The pearls usually have a low or very low luster and may look milky. Some thin-coated pearls, however, may show a decent medium luster.

♦ The nacre coating has cracks.

♦ Areas are visible where the nacre has peeled off.

♦ Layers of the shell beads are slightly visible when the pearls are suspended and light shines through them. These layers look like curved lines, stripes or wood grain. Usually the thinner the nacre, the easier it is to see the lines. Figure 4.5 is an example of what the shell layers look like in a thinly-coated pearl with light shining through it.

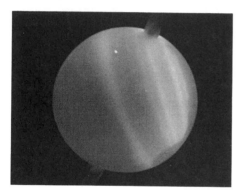

Fig. 4.5 Thin-nacre cultured pearl with light shining through it. Note shell nucleus layers.

Fig. 4.6 Light and dark views of mother-of-pearl shell beads

If you can't see any shell layers, this does not mean that the nacre is thick. There are lots of thinly-coated pearls that don't show these layers. However, if you can see them, the nacre is probably too thin.

♦ As the beads are rolled, some may look light and then dark as the light shines through them. This is because the shell beads may have mother-of-pearl layers that block the light. This phenomenon is called "blinking" and can sometimes be seen in thinly coated pearls. Figure 4.6 is an example of two shell beads with no nacre. One in the light position and one in the dark position. When rotated, each of these pearls "blinks." Pearls with thick nacre should not blink.

A more accurate way of judging nacre thickness is by examining the drill holes of the pearls, preferably with a 10-power magnifier such as a hand loupe (fig. 4.7). (If you are seriously interested in gems, you should own a fully-corrected, 10-power, triplet loupe. You can buy

them at jewelry or gem supply stores. Plan on paying at least $25 for a good loupe. Examining drill holes with a loupe will also help you detect dyes and imitations). The drill-hole method is too slow to be practical for dealers, but it is a good way for less-skilled people to estimate nacre thickness. It also allows appraisers to give a more objective measure of nacre thickness. Figures 4.8 - 4.11 give you an idea of what drill holes look like under magnification.

Fig. 4.7 A loupe

If you have some pearls at home, try examining their drill holes with a loupe under a good light. Find the dividing line between the nacre and the bead. Then look at a millimeter ruler with the loupe to get a visual image of a 0.35-mm thickness. Compare this thickness to that of the nacre. If it is less, this is a sign your pearls are too thin. Seeing actual examples of thin, medium, and thick nacres is an easier way to learn to tell the difference, but examples of each may be hard for you to find.

This book suggests 0.35 mm as a minimum because the GIA uses it as a dividing point between thin and medium nacre and because it has been mentioned in the trade as a minimum. For example, Hiroshi Komatsu of the Tokyo Mikimoto research lab is quoted as saying, "Our tests show the best luster and color occur with at least 0.35 mm of nacre, and Mikimoto pearls are always thicker" (as quoted by Frank Ward in the August 1985 issue of *National Geographic*). Keep in mind that the nacre thickness may not be the same throughout a pearl. Nacre measurements can also vary depending on the measuring instrument used and the person doing the measuring. So consider the 0.35-mm minimum as an approximate thickness.

Nacre thickness has been one of the most discussed issues in the pearl industry. In their December 1991 quarterly bulletin, the Gemmological Association and Gem Testing Laboratory of Great Britain announced they have started issuing nacre thickness reports. This is due to requests from the British Association of Cultured Pearl Importers. They have been concerned about the low-quality, very-thin-nacre pearls that are flooding the market and don't want the reputation of the trade to be tarnished.

Fig. 4.8 Pearl with acceptable nacre thickness. Note the dividing line between the lighter nacre and the darker nucleus.

Fig. 4.9 Pearl with acceptable nacre thickness. Often the drill hole is small, so it's hard to see the dividing line.

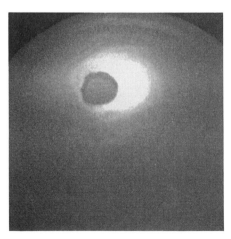

Fig. 4.10 Pearl with nacre that is too thin

Fig. 4.11 Pearl with nacre so thin it is peeling off

When you have your pearls appraised, be sure to ask if nacre thickness is indicated on the report. Also ask how the appraiser's nacre-thickness categories are defined in terms of millimeter thickness. A term such as "thin" can vary from one person to another, so definitions are necessary.

Also make sure that the millimeter thickness is of the radius of the pearl, not of the diameter, which would be twice the nacre thickness along the radius. If someone tells you the average nacre thickness of an Akoya pearl is 1 mm, figure they have doubled it. Today it's hard to find Akoya pearls with even a 0.5-mm thickness.

It's not deceptive to sell thin-nacre pearls as long as the thin nacre and its consequences are disclosed to buyers. Ideally, consumers could choose from a wide range of nacre thicknesses and know exactly what they were getting for their money. Since this ideal does not currently exist, it's to your advantage to pay attention to nacre thickness and to learn to detect thin nacre yourself.

Is Nacre Thickness Important and Does it Affect Pricing?

As you shop, you may encounter pearl salespeople who claim nacre thickness is unimportant and has no effect upon price. Beware. All their pearls may be of low quality. Ask them, "Why is something which affects the beauty and durability of my pearls unimportant?"

As for price, it has to be affected by nacre thickness. It naturally will cost a farmer progressively more to culture pearls for 6 months, 1 1/2 years and 2 1/2 years. The additional cost must be passed on to the buyers.

Often the effect of nacre thickness on price is linked to that of luster. Thicker nacre usually means higher luster, and both bring higher prices. An example of this linkage is found in the pearl pricing system of the Adachi America Co. They don't list nacre thickness as a separate factor on their price guides; but whenever it is lower than the luster grade indicates, they'll downgrade the luster and sell the pearls for less. To them nacre thickness is important.

The Mikimoto Company thinks it is important too. One of their advisors, Shigeru Miki, made the following statement in the August 1985 National Geographic article by Frank Ward. "The most important quality of a cultured pearl is thickness of the nacre. It gives color, luster, and appearance. Pearls are among the softest of all gems, and normal body fluids, as well as contact with perfumes, hair sprays, and acids reduce nacre. A thinly coated pearl won't last many years."

Golay Buchel, a company with branches in Europe, North America and the Orient, discusses luster and nacre thickness in its booklet *Pearls*. They are listed as separate value factors and both are described as important. Golay Buchel's advice to consumers (p. 34): "Remain flexible with regards to colour, size, shape and light surface markings, but **never** make concessions regarding the thickness of the coating."

Chapter 6 Quiz

Select the correct answer.

1. A jeweler says his pearls are AAA quality. You should conclude:

a. The pearls are of high quality.
b. The pearls may be of any quality
c. The pearls are not graded properly because the highest possible grade is A+.
d. The pearls have a high luster. Quality factors such as shape and color also need to be indicated.

2. A large percentage of the Akoya pearls sold today:

a. have a very high luster.
b. have thick or very thick nacre.
c. have thin or very thin nacre.
d. none of the above.

3. You have a written appraisal that states your pearl necklace has very thick nacre. You should assume:

a. Your pearls have a nacre thickness of exactly .5 mm or more on all the pearls
b. Your pearls have a nacre thickness of approximately .5 mm or more on all pearls.
c. Your pearls have a nacre thickness of approximately .5 mm or more on most pearls of the strand
d. Nothing if the appraiser has not defined his/her nacre-thickness grades somewhere on the appraisal.

4. Which type of lighting will make pearls look the most lustrous?

a. a bare 100-watt light bulb
b. candlelight
c. daylight on a rainy day
d. a fluorescent light covered with a translucent plastic shade

True or False?

5. Today, cultured pearls tend to have thicker nacre than they did in the 1950's.

6. When the judging luster of a strand, you should roll the pearls slightly on a flat, white surface.

7. If a cultured pearl is left in an Akoya oyster for at least three years, it will have a high luster.

8. Pearls with very low luster are easy to spot because they look more like white beads than pearls.

9. There's no point in paying $35 for a loupe when you can find brand new ones for $10.

10. If a pearl has thick nacre, it will have a high luster.

Answers:

1. b There's no standardized pearl grading system, so a jeweler can assign whatever meaning he wants to a grade. Even standardized grades such as those for diamonds are misused and inflated by some salespeople. Therefore it's best to base your judgement of a gem on what it looks like rather than on a grade assigned to it.

2. c

3. d The grading of nacre thickness is not standardized. "Very thick nacre" can have a variety of meanings depending on which appraiser or jeweler is using the term.

4. a

5. F

6. T

7. F Not necessarily. Improper cultivation techniques, disease, and pollution are a few of the factors that can lower the luster of a pearl even though it is left in an Akoya oyster for a long period of time.

8. T

9. F A $10 loupe will generally distort what it magnifies. A 10-power, fully corrected loupe is an ideal gem magnifier. Unfortunately, it will cost more than $10 brand new.

10 F Not necessarily. South Sea pearls usually have thicker nacre than Akoya pearls, yet their luster tends to be lower. The quality of the nacre is just as important as its thickness. A pearl with very thick nacre can have a very low luster.

5

Judging Color

If you were buying Swiss cheese and you had a choice between some that was white and some that was slightly yellow or cream color, which would you choose? Most likely the cream color because the average person has been conditioned to expect Swiss cheese to have a yellowish tint. If when you bought Swiss cheese, you happened to discover that pieces with large holes often tasted better than those without, you might also develop a preference for Swiss cheese with big holes.

People's expectation of what pearls should look like have been conditioned in a similar manner. Many expect pearls to be white because that is what they are accustomed to seeing. Plus pearls are associated with the moon, weddings, purity--which, in turn, are connected to the color white.

Within the jewelry trade, it was also noticed that Akoya or Persian Gulf pearls with high luster often had a pinkish tint. So, a lot of people developed a preference for pearls with a slight pink tint. To meet the demand for such pearls, producers bleached their pearls and dyed them pink.

Coloring foods to enhance their appearance is an accepted practice, so is bleaching pearls. Dyeing pearls, however, has not been as well accepted, especially if the resulting color is unstable. Sometimes higher prices are charged for dyed pearls. Some people are opposed to this practice.

This chapter discusses factors to consider when choosing the color of pearls. The topic of color will also be addressed in the chapters on freshwater, black, and South Sea pearls. The Akoya pearl is the main focus of this chapter.

Pearl Color

Pearl color is complex. It's a combination of the following:

Body Color   The predominant basic color of the pearl.

Overtone   The one or more colors that overlie the body color. On black pearls these colors are easiest to see in the lighter areas of the pearl. On white pearls they are easier to see in the darker areas.

     For example, lay some white pearls on something white and look at them under a strong, direct light (midday sun is ideal). The outer rim area of the pearls, which is reflecting the white background, will be lighter than the center of the pearls if they are of decent quality (except for the bright reflection of the light). If you look closely, you should see a slight pink, green, and/or silver color in the central dark areas of the pearls. This is the overtone. Generally you will see more than one overtone color in a strand of pearls (see color photo #2). You may also see more than one on the same pearl. For example, the South Sea pearl on the front cover of this book has both pink and green overtones. So do some of the pearls in color photo #2.

Iridescence   A play of lustrous colors. They may be like those of the rainbow, or they may be a subtle combination of colors such as pink, blue, green, and silver. (See color photo #7, the mabe-oyster blister pearl. The colors of this pearl change when you move it in your hand.)

     Orient is another term that is used to refer to pearl iridescence. In a handout from their pearl grading course, the GIA specifies that "orient has 6 colors: violet, blue, red, green, yellow, orange, all the colors of the rainbow." Some dealers, however, employ the term more loosely to also mean a combination of overtone colors. Other dealers and many books written in the past use the term "orient" to refer to luster because iridescence and luster are interconnected. Since "orient" may be interpreted in various ways, this book tends to use the term "iridescence" instead.

When you shop for pearls, you may come across terms such as **white rosé**. This means white pearls with a pink overtone. "Rose" is the French word for pink. **Pink rosé** means that most of the pearls have a pink body color and a pink overtone. White pearls with a silver overtone may be described as **silver(y) white**. Often salespeople don't specify the overtone but they just say one color such as "pink" which describes their overall impression of the pearls.

Judging Pearl Color

When deciding what color pearls to buy, your primary concern should be what looks best on you. But you will also want to know how the color affects their price.

The overall body color is the main determinant of the price. Five main **body color categories** for pearls are:

Pink Often the highest price category, but some dealers price pink and white pearls alike. A few dealers make a distinction between pearls with subtle pink tints and those that look artificial and obviously dyed. They may refuse to stock the latter. Incidently, jewelers often have no way of knowing if their pink pearls are dyed because suppliers are not required to disclose this. If the pearls are pink, just assume they might have been dyed. (In the August 1985 issue of *National Geographic*, there is a good article on pearls by Frank Ward which has a more detailed discussion about pearl dyeing.)

White Equal to or less than pink pearls. Some people in the trade have a negative view of "white pearls" because they associate them with the very thin-nacre pearls that look milky white and have no overtone. White pearls can be very lustrous and valuable. Calling high-luster pearls silvery white is one way to distinguish between high- and low- quality white pearls.

Light Cream Usually less than white. The higher the quality of the pearls, the greater the price difference will probably be between light cream and white. In low qualities there may be no difference.

Cream Usually less than light cream. In cream colors, the general tendency is the darker the color, the less it will cost. Cream-color pearls are sometimes termed **champagne pearls**.

Dark Cream or Golden May be priced about 40% or more lower than white pearls. The darker the cream or yellow color, the greater the price difference.

When judging color, keep in mind that there is no standardized system of communicating or grading color in the pearl industry. What one dealer calls light cream, another might call cream. Nevertheless, there is an awareness of the concept "cream color" and general agreement that cream-color Akoya pearls tend to cost less than those which are pink and white.

The **overtone** may or may not affect the price. There are three basic overtones--pink, green, and silver (blue, purple, and gold are sometimes listed too). If overtone has an effect, it will be as follows:

Pink overtone Sometimes may increase the price slightly

Silver Usually no effect

Green Sometimes may decrease the price slightly

There's no need to be too concerned about overtone. For one thing, pearl strands tend to consist of a combination of overtones, but on better quality strands, the differences are more subtle. For another, there is no general agreement in the trade as to how overtones affect price. Most dealers, however, would probably concede that Akoya pearls with pink overtones tend to be more highly valued than those with green ones. This explains why pearls are often dyed pink but not green. What counts most about overtone is how it affects your overall impression of the color of the pearls.

The third color component of pearls, **iridescence**, is rarely obvious on round Akoya pearls. It tends to be very subtle. A more obvious iridescence--flashes of rainbow colors--is more likely to be seen on freshwater pearls and baroque shapes. Iridescence is always considered a positive value factor.

When examining pearls for color remember the following tips:

♦ Judge the color of pearls against a non-reflective white background. Pearls not only reflect the color of the background, they also absorb it. Afterwards, place the pearls on your hand or around your neck to see how they look on you.

♦ Take into consideration the lighting (see next section). If possible look at the pearls under different types of light sources--daylight near a window, fluorescent, and incandescent (light bulbs). You'll probably be wearing the pearls under a variety of light sources.

♦ It's a lot easier to compare color than to remember it. If possible, wear or take along some comparison pearls. Otherwise, compare it to other pearls in the store. Even using white and cream-colored papers as color references is better than relying on color memory.

♦ When pearl strands are exactly adjacent, their color may seem to bleed from one strand to another. Therefore, also compare them slightly separated from each other.

♦ Every now and then, look away from the pearls at other colors and objects. When you focus on one color too long, your perception of it becomes distorted.

♦ Consider how evenly distributed the color is on the pearl(s), especially if it's one major pearl on a ring or pendant. A uniform color is more highly valued than a blotchy one.

♦ If you are trying to decide between white and pink pearls of the same quality but the pink pearls cost more. Look in a few of the drill holes with a 10-power magnifier. If you can see red or pink stains on the nacre layer or a pink line between the nacre and the bead nucleus, they are dyed (color photo #4). Seeing positive indications of dye may influence your decision. By the way, even if you don't see evidence of dye, the pearls may still be dyed.

♦ Make sure you're alert and feel good when you examine pearls. If you're tired, sick, or under the influence of alcohol or drugs, your perception of color will be impaired.

How Lighting Affects Color

Just as luster is affected by lighting, so is color, but in a different way. If you were to take a photograph indoors under a light bulb with daylight film, the picture would be orangy or yellowish. If you took it under fluorescent light, the picture would look greenish. Even though, unlike cameras, your eyes can adjust to changes of color from lighting, you are still influenced by them. Consequently, your perception of pearl color will depend on the lighting the pearls are viewed under.

The whitest, most neutral light is at midday. Besides adding the least amount of color, this light makes it easier to see various nuances of color. Consequently, it's best to judge pearl color under a daylight-equivalent light. Day-light fluorescent bulbs approximate this ideal, but some of these lights are better than others. One that is often recommended for color grading gems is the Duro-Test Vita Lite. This light, however, is not as effective as true sunlight for seeing detail. For example, it is normally easier to read very fine print in sunlight than in artificial light. The intensity of the light from the sun has a lot to do with this.

When you shop for pearls, your choice of lighting will probably be limited. Use the information below to help you compensate for improper lighting.

Type of light	Effect of Light
Light bulbs up to 150 watts candlelight	Add red or orange, so pearls may look pinker or more yellowish
Fluorescent lights	Depends on what type they are. Some have a neutral effect. Others add green which may make the pearls look greenish or grayish.
Light under overcast sky or in the shade under blue sky	Adds blue so pearls may look grayish or a bit bluish
Sunlight	Depends on the time of day, the season of the year, and the geographic location. At midday it normally has a neutral effect on the color. Earlier and later in the day it adds red, orange, or yellow so the pearls may look pinker or more yellowish.

Emphasis on proper lighting when viewing gems has not been restricted to modern-day times. In 1908, in *The Book of the Pearl* (p. 370), Kunz and Stevenson wrote:
"At great receptions, large and apparently magnificent pearls are frequently seen, which are really of inferior quality, and yet owing to the absence of pure daylight,

they can easily be mistaken for perfect specimens by any one not especially familiar with pearls. Indeed, if the royalties of Europe should wear all the pearls belonging to the crown jewels at the same time, in a palace or hall lighted with candles, gas, or even with some types of electric light, they would seem to have a quality which many of them do not and never did possess. It is, therefore, essential for the buyer to use every precaution in reference to the light in which he examines his purchase."

What Causes Pearl Color?

A lot of pearl farmers wish they had the full answer to this question. Then they could control the color of the pearls they cultivated. Now they have only part answers or clues. Some of the determinants of pearl color seem to be:

♦ The type of host oyster. Oysters vary in their potential to produce certain colored pearls. For example, black pearls are cultivated in the black-lip oyster because other oysters don't produce pearls of the same type. Even though pearl farmers know the black-lip oyster is essential to the cultivation of black pearls, they don't know yet how to consistently make it produce a specific color. The pearl may end up being white or a variety of shades of gray as well as black, bronze, greenish or purplish.

♦ The quality of the nacre. If the nacre is very thin, the color will look milky and lack overtone tints. Besides being affected by the number of layers of nacre, pearl color is affected by the thickness of each layer. In *Pearls of the World* (p. 71), researcher Koji Wada states, "The reason why the pearl made by the Akoya pearl-oyster has a better pink tone than pearls made by other mollusks is that it has layers of equal thickness."

♦ The environment they are grown in. It's theorized that there may be trace elements in the water that affect the color. For example, cream-color pearls are typical of natural pearls from the Ohio River, but not of those found in other American Rivers.

♦ The color of the tissue that is inserted with the bead nucleus. (Tissue from another oyster's mantle, the part of the oyster that secretes pearl nacre, has to be implanted with the shell bead for a cultured pearl to grow.) Koji Wada has found that if the tissue inserted in Akoya oysters is yellow, cream-colored pearls tend to form. If white, white pearls result (*Modern Jeweler*, September 1990, pp. 42-44, David Federman).

What Color is Best for You?

Most pearl experts agree that a buyer's color choice should be primarily based on what will look good on the person who will wear the pearls. Some salespeople, though, give color advice by suggesting what's popular in specific geographic areas. One fairly consistent statement, for example, is that South Americans prefer cream- or golden-colored pearls.

When shopping in the United States, the color listed as the number one choice may vary from one salesperson to another. Perhaps it's a matter of what the store has in stock. Quite often it's claimed that the most popular pearl color in America is pink. The US, however, is a diverse nation. Consequently, pink is not the color that looks best on all Americans. Picking a color on the basis of its popularity might lead to a poor choice.

Determining the colors that flatter you most is not always easy. Carole Jackson, in her book, *Color Me Beautiful*, provides some guidelines with color illustrations. She points out on page 28, for example, that olive-skinned people and most blacks and Orientals look radiant in clear, vivid, cool colors (pink, white, blue, red) but sallow in warm colors (cream, orange, beige, mustard). Warm colors, however, are very flattering to people with peach or golden complexions (Redheads and blondes often have this skin coloring).

Some people in the trade recommend white and pink pearls to Asians and Anglos and cream or golden pearls to blacks and olive-skinned customers. This is because cream colors look whiter on a dark-skinned person than on someone with lighter skin.

One easy way to determine which pearl colors will compliment you is to put on white, light pink, and cream-colored clothing and see what looks best next to your face. It's helpful to get the opinion of family and friends. Often, two of the colors look equally attractive, but it's rare that all three will. The final test will be to put the pearls on your hand or around your neck and see how they look. Consider, too, if you want people to notice the pearls when you wear them. If you do, then choose a color that contrasts with your skin tone. Pearls that blend in too closely won't be very striking.

When you are buying for others, they probably won't be able to try on the pearls. So beforehand, observe what color clothes they like to wear and look good in. If they don't like beige or cream-colored clothes and these colors don't flatter them, you would be better off avoiding cream-colored pearls.

Two other considerations when choosing pearl color are versatility and price. If you would like to wear the pearls as often as possible, then select a color that will go well with most of your wardrobe. If your budget is limited and you are trying to choose between light or dark cream pearls, the dark cream pearls could be the ideal choice. Don't buy them, though, if cream colors make you look washed out. The purpose of jewelry is to enhance your appearance, not detract from it. So put some thought into your color choices. It will pay off in the end.

Chapter 5 Quiz

Select the correct answer.

1. Which of the following body colors is considered the most valuable for an Akoya pearl?

   a. gold
   b. pink
   c. cream
   d. champagne

2. Which of the following overtone colors is the most valued on an Akoya pearl?

   a. green
   b. blue
   c. gold
   d. pink

3. You look in a drill hole of pearl and you see a dark pink line between the nacre and the bead nucleus, this means:

   a. The pearl comes from the pink-lip oyster.
   b. Nothing in particular. It's an inherent characteristic of pearls with pink overtones.
   c. The pearl has been dyed.

4. When judging the color of pearls, you should examine them

   a. on a black background.
   b. on a white background.
   c. on a background the same color as their body color.
   d. hanging in the air.

5. Which type of light is best for viewing pearl overtones?

   a. sunlight at midday
   a. daylight under an overcast sky
   c. fluorescent light
   d. incandescent light bulb

6. Which of the following can affect your perception of pearl color?

   a. The color of the room you are in
   b. The lighting
   c. Alcoholic beverages
   d. All of the above

Answers:

1. b

2. d

3. c

4. b

5. a

6. d

6

Judging Flaws

Imagine that you're buying a bouquet of roses for a special friend. If you were to look closely at each rose, you would probably notice some brown spots, small holes, or torn edges. Yet it's doubtful that any of these flaws would keep you from getting the bouquet. You would select it on the basis of its overall attractiveness.

However, if you were buying just one rose for somebody, you would most likely examine it more closely and expect it to have fewer flaws than the roses in a bouquet. Judging pearls is much the same. Our standards of perfection for a single pearl are normally higher than for a strand. But whether we are dealing with roses or pearls, we should expect nature to leave some sort of autograph.

When discussing flaws in diamonds or colored gems, the jewelry trade uses the term **clarity**. This refers to the flaw grade or the degree to which a stone is flawed. In the pearl industry, a variety of terms is used. For example:

Blemish	Spotting
Cleanliness or Cleanness	Surface
Complexion	Surface appearance
Flawlessness	Surface perfection
Purity	Texture

There are also a variety of synonyms for the term flaw:

Blemish
Imperfection
Irregularity
Surface characteristic
Surface mark or marking

When dealing with diamonds and colored stones, gemologists limit the term "blemish" to surface flaws such as scratches and bumps. The term "inclusion" refers to flaws that extend below the surface such as cracks and holes.

"**Blemish**" takes on a different meaning when used with pearls. It means any kind of flaw, internal or external. This book normally uses the term "flaw" because it's short and easily understood by the trade and general public. For the sake of variety, some of the other terms are used as well.

Flaws can be positive features. They serve as identifying marks that a gem is ours and not somebody else's. They help prove that it is real and not imitation. Flaws can lower the price of gems without affecting their overall beauty. Perfection does not seem to be a goal of nature. In fact, the longer a pearl is in an oyster, the more likely it is for irregularities to occur. Therefore, when shopping for pearls, there's no need to look for flawless ones. You just need to know what types of flaws to avoid. This chapter will go into that, but first you should know what flaws are found on pearls.

Pearl Flaws

A standardized terminology has not been developed for pearl flaws. The terms found below are based mostly on those listed in the GIA (Gemological Institute of America) pearl grading course. These flaws are usually judged without magnification.

♦ **Bumps and Welts:** Raised areas which are found alone or in groups (fig. 6.1 & 6.2). They may sometimes cover most of the surface area of the pearl. If bumps or welts are very large, they can put the pearl into the off-round category. Occasionally pearls have a wrinkled appearance. This is due to groupings of welts (fig. 6.3).

♦ **Discolorations:** Spotty areas often caused from concentrations of conchiolin, a protein substance that holds nacre crystals together. Discolorations are not frequently seen because pearls are typically bleached to even out their color.

♦ **Chips, Holes, and Patches of Missing Nacre:** Flaws which may occur on any type of pearl but that are particularly common on those with thin nacre (fig 6.5).

♦ **Pits and Pinpoints:** Tiny holes on the surface which are normally hardly noticeable and, therefore, not serious (fig. 6.7). "Pinpoints" may also refer to tiny bumps since, from a distance, these look about the same as tiny pits.

♦ **Dimples:** Circular depressions or indentations which are often found in groups.

♦ **Dull Spots:** Areas of very low luster due to variations in nacre quality or contact with chemicals, cosmetics, or skin secretions.

Fig. 6.1 Bump

Fig. 6.2 Insignificant pinpoint-size bump

Fig. 6.3 Welts ("wrinkles")

Fig. 6.4 Cracked nacre

Fig. 6.5 Missing nacre

Fig. 6.6 Minor scratches

♦ **Cracks:** Breaks in the nacre and/or bead nucleus (fig 6.4). Small cracks in the bead may look like little hairs trapped under the nacre. Cracks, even when not visible, can threaten the durability of a pearl.

♦ **Scratches:** Straight or crooked lines scraped on the pearl (fig. 6.6). These aren't serious unless the pearl is so badly scratched the luster and beauty is affected.

Determining Which Flaws Are Acceptable and Which Aren't

It's not the presence of flaws that matters. It's the type, quantity, and prominence of the flaws that does. Listed below are flaws which would normally be considered unacceptable:

♦ **Cracks throughout the pearls**. Thick nacre does not crack easily. Thin nacre does. Even if the cracks aren't noticeable, they are a sign that the nacre is too thin and that the pearls won't give you lasting wear.

♦ **Prominent flaws in a single pearl**. When buying pearl earrings, pendants, pins, or rings, pay closer attention to the flaws. For example, the pearl with the bump in figure 6.1 would not be acceptable as the featured pearl of a jewelry piece, but it would be okay in a strand. If you are buying a large expensive pearl and you want to compromise on price, try to select one whose flaws can be hidden by the setting.

♦ **Patches of missing nacre**. Just as diamonds with big chips are considered unacceptable, so are pearls with chunks of missing nacre. Both the beauty and durability of the pearl are affected.

♦ **Obvious discolorations throughout the pearls**. For the sake of beauty, try to select pearls with a uniform color. There are plenty of them available.

Fig. 6.7 A group of minor pits

Fig. 6.8 A group of tiny welts

♦ **Flaws which cover the majority of the surface of the pearl.** They can cause a viewer's attention to be directed more at the flaws than at the pearls. Figures 6.7 and 6.8 are examples of how groups of minor flaws over a large surface area become more noticeable and therefore less acceptable.

Despite the undesirability of blemishes, if you had to choose between heavily flawed, lustrous pearls and near flawless pearls with very thin nacre and low luster, you would be better off with the flawed ones. At least you would be getting some pearl for your money.

Drawing a line between what's acceptable and what isn't is not always easy. Below are a couple of examples that may help you understand what is meant by "unacceptable quality." Both of these strands are low quality. For many people and occasions, strand A would still be acceptable, whereas it's hard to imagine why anyone would ever want to buy strand B. Nacre has already peeled off of three of the pearls on strand B. The overall luster is very low and two of the pearls seem to have no luster at all. It's obvious, too, from looking at the missing nacre areas that the nacre thickness is very low. In sum, strand B is just made up of shell beads with a bit of an ugly nacre coating.

Fig. 6.9 Strand A: Acceptable or unacceptable quality depending on the buyer's goals

Fig. 6.10 Strand B: Unacceptable quality

Strand A has a fair number of flaws, but they aren't very noticeable, especially when it is worn. It has a medium-nacre thickness, which can be determined by looking in the drill holes. It's luster ranges between medium and low (it looks lower in the photo because of the diffused lighting), and the pearls are fairly round. For somebody with a limited budget, this strand could be a good choice. For someone looking for a fine quality necklace for a special person, Strand A would be unacceptable.

Fig. 6.11 Strand A: Enlarged view

Fig. 6.12 Strand B: Enlarged view

Keep in mind when buying pearls that it's not just their inherent quality that determines their acceptability. Your needs and desires also count. Therefore, it's you that has the final say as to what's acceptable and what's not.

Tips On Judging Flaws

When you shop for diamonds, salespeople may suggest that you look at the stone under magnification so you'll know it's clarity. This won't happen when you shop for pearls. The reason jewelers don't have you view them under a microscope is because pearls are graded and valued on the basis of how they look to the naked eye, not under magnification (except nacre thickness).

When dealing with knowledgeable salespeople that have your interests at heart, you won't need to look at pearls with a loupe (hand magnifier). They will point out the flaws and other quality factors and show you how to compare pearls. But there are times, when it is advisable to use a loupe. Some are:

♦ **When dealing with people you don't know or who may not be trustworthy.** Suppose you are at a flea market or an antique show and you see a pearl piece you'd love to have that you would never find in a jewelry store. Or, suppose you are on vacation abroad and you

70

want a souvenir but you don't know any jewelers and none have been recommended to you. In both cases, it would be advisable to use a loupe and check for flaws, thin nacre, dye, and imitations. The more experience you get at examining a pearl's flaws, surface, and drill holes with a loupe, the easier it will be for you to identify them and judge their quality.

♦ **When the lighting is poor.** Suppose you're an antique dealer or a pawnbroker and you're in a place where the lighting is not ideal. And suppose you have to make a quick decision about whether to buy some pearls and how much to offer. Poor lighting will make it harder to judge flaws and overall quality. Use a loupe as a means of compensating for the lack of proper lighting.

♦ **If you have a hard time reading small print.** It's not any easier to see small flaws with the naked eye than it is to read fine print. When buying top quality pearls, a quick look at them through a loupe could help you make a better choice.

♦ **Whenever pearls are being offered at a price that seems too good to be true.** There's usually a catch somewhere. It will probably be easier to find it with a loupe than with the unaided eye, especially for people who don't deal with pearls on a regular basis.

A few other pointers for judging flaws are listed below:

♦ Besides looking at the pearls against a white background, look at them against a dark one. Certain flaws show up better against black or other dark colors. Also hold the pearls in the air to examine them for flaws. Do not judge luster or color in this way though.

♦ Examine the pearls under a strong light. The more intense the light, the easier it is to see detail. When judging blemish, it's also a good idea to look at pearls under different types of lighting--barc/diffuscd, fluorescent/incandescent, close/distant. Each type may bring out different details in the pearls.

♦ Roll the pearls. Otherwise you may not see some serious flaws and you won't know what percentage of the pearls is flawed. An anecdote by Kunz & Stevenson in *The Book of the Pearl* (p. 371) illustrates the importance of looking at all sides of the pearls.

> "A pearl necklace valued at $200,000, shown at one of our recent great expositions, was, to all appearances, a remarkably beautiful collection, and it was only when the intending purchaser took them from their velvet bed and held them in his hands that he realized that there was not a perfect pearl in the entire collection. It must have taken more than a week of study for the clever dealer to arrange them so that the best part, sometimes the only good part of each pearl, should be where the eye would fall upon it. After they had been turned in the hands a few seconds, not one perfect specimen was visible."

♦ Keep in mind that it's normal for pearls to have a few flaws. The GIA takes this into consideration in the way they dcfine their "flawless" category for pearls on a strand: "Most appear blemish-free to the unaided eye." It would be abnormal for all of the pearls to be flawless.

Do we need standardized grades to judge flaws?

The diamond industry has a standardized system for grading flaws based on a system developed by the GIA. Ten-power magnification is used. The advantage of having this system is that buyers can communicate what they want anywhere in the world. In addition, written appraisals and quality reports are more meaningful.

The pearl industry does not have such a system. Nevertheless, flaws do affect the price of pearls. Occasionally you will come across grades such as AAA, AA, A. Depending on the supplier or store, these grades may refer to the luster, the flaws, a combination of these two factors, or they may include other factors such as shape and nacre thickness. In essence, pearl grades have no meaning except what the seller assigns to them. Therefore, do not rely on grades to compare pearl prices. (Don't rely on grades to compare diamond prices either because the grades are often misused).

One of the drawbacks of the diamond grading system is that it has sometimes led buyers to become so focused on color and clarity that they overlook brilliance and cut. Internationally recognized grading documents also neglect these factors somewhat. They often don't mention the proportions of the bottom and top of the diamond (pavilion depth and crown height percentages). Yet these proportions can significantly affect the beauty and value of your diamond.

The lack of standardized flaw grades in the pearl industry has perhaps led to a greater emphasis on brilliance (luster). If so, this is fortunate. The lack of standardization has not kept pearl dealers from judging blemish, nor should it keep you from doing so. You can form your own grading system.

Maybe you'd like to have three grades like A, B, & C. If you are accustomed to the grades A, B, C, D, & F from school, these may be easier to use. Whenever you look at pearls, ask to see a wide range of qualities. Some stores may have master strands indicating different qualities and these will be helpful. Gradually you will be able to create your own mental image of each grade category. Base your set of blemish grades on:

♦ The prominence of the flaws. Visible flaws away from drill holes are more serious than those near the holes. High bumps can be more noticeable than small pits or low bumps.

♦ The type of flaws. Chipped or missing nacre is usually more serious than bumps even though it may be less noticeable.

♦ The percentage of the pearl surface that is flawed. It's a lot more serious if 80% of the surface of a pearl is flawed than if only 10% of it is. You need to roll the pearls to check this factor.

♦ The percentage of pearls on a strand that are flawed and to what degree. This is a factor that doesn't exist in diamond grading. Pearl grading is more complex. It's much harder to develop consistent grades for sets of gems than for single gems.

After you've established your own grading system and can use it consistently, you'll be better able to compare prices than if you just rely on grades written on pearl tags--grades whose meaning changes according to the store or supplier using them. Another benefit of creating your own grading system--the most important one--you will increase your powers of observation and thought. This is what pearl evaluation is all about.

Chapter 6 Quiz

Select the correct answer.

1. Which of the following is the least serious?

a. missing nacre
b. a crack
c. a scratch
d. a large discoloration

2. Which of the following can affect the way you grade the flaws on a strand of pearls?

a. The background the pearls are viewed against
b. The lighting
c. Your eyesight
d. All of the above

3. Which is the least serious?

a. A bump next to a drill hole
b. A visible discoloration on a single pearl
c. A group of welts
d. A cracked bead nucleus

4. Flaws:

a. Can help you prove that your pearls are real and not imitation.
b. Can lower the price of pearls without affecting their overall beauty.
c. Can help you distinguish your pearls from those of someone else.
d. All of the above.

True or False?

5. When checking for flaws on a strand, you should roll the pearls in order to see their entire surface.

6. Pearl flaws should never be examined under magnification.

7. The longer a pearl is in an oyster, the more likely it is to have flaws.

8. The term "pearl blemish" only refers to flaws that are on the surface of a pearl.

9. Pearls with flaws are defective.

Answers:

1. c

2. d

3. a

4. d.

5. T

6. F Even though pearl flaws are graded without magnification, a magnifier can help you compensate for poor lighting or poor eyesight. Also, knowing what pearl flaws look like under magnification can help you determine if "pearls" are imitation or not.

7. T

8. F It can also refer to internal flaws such as cracked nuclei and flaws that extend below the surface such as holes and missing nacre. The term "surface characteristic" can also mean internal flaw when it is applied to pearls.

9. F It's normal for pearls to have flaws.

7

Size, Weight, Length

Size

Suppose you are in a store looking at 3 strands of Akoya pearls that were all bought from the same dealer at the same time. Their sizes and prices are:

a. 3 - 3 1/2 mm --- $350
b. 4 1/2 - 5 mm --- $350
c. 6 - 6 1/2 mm --- $700

Would it be surprising if they were all the same color and quality?

Not necessarily, some dealers do price 3 - 5 mm strands alike in some of their grades. Other dealers would increase the price for all their grades as size gets bigger. But every dealer would show a price increase from 5 mm to 6 1/2 mm, although the degree of increase could vary a great deal. There is no standardized system for determining exactly how pearl size affects price. Nevertheless, pearl dealers would agree that size is a very important price factor.

The size of round saltwater cultured pearls is expressed in terms of their diameter measured in millimeters. One millimeter is about 1/25 of an inch. Since pearl size varies within a strand, a range of 1/2 millimeter is usually indicated, e.g. 7 - 7 1/2 mm. Occasionally, a few of the pearls might fall slightly above or below the size indicated.

The size of non-round pearls can be expressed in terms of their greatest width and length and in some cases depth. The measurements are generally rounded to the nearest half or whole millimeter.

Fig. 7.1 Millimeter sizes. Diagram by Dawn King.

When determining the effect of size on price, keep in mind the following.

♦ Price jumps between pearl sizes tend to be uneven. An illustration of this is the following imaginary price list for grade X pearls.

7 1/2 - 8	$2,500
8 - 8 1/2	$5,000
8 1/2 - 9	$6,000
9 - 9 1/2	11,000

The above price increments are not unusual. Pearl prices tend to jump more as the sizes reach the 8 or 9 mm mark.

♦ Price/size relationships vary from one dealer to another.

♦ The effect of size on price varies from one harvest to another. If too many pearls of one size are harvested, their price will go down.

♦ Size tends to have the least effect on price in sizes below 5 mm.

♦ Demand can have an important impact on the way size affects price. If there's a high demand for a specific size, its price tends to increase. This explains why occasionally smaller pearls sell for more than bigger ones of the same quality.

Weight

When pearl dealers buy large lots of cultured pearls, they are usually charged according to the weight of the pearls. The measure generally used is the **momme**, an ancient Japanese unit of weight which equals 3.75 grams or 18.75 carats. **Kan** is a Japanese unit of weight equalling 1000 momme. Pearls are not sold by the momme or kan in retail stores.

The size of natural pearls is often expressed in pearl grains. One **grain** equals 0.25 carat. Natural American freshwater pearls may be sold according to their carat weight. The **gram** is commonly used to express the weight of cultured freshwater pearls, although carat weight is also used. One **carat** = 1/5 gram. Or in other words 5 carats = 1 gram. Weight equivalences are summarized in Table 7.1.

Table 7.1 Weight Conversions	
1 carat (ct)	= 0.2 g = 0.007 oz av = 4 p grains = 0.053 m
1 gram (g)	= 5 cts = 0.035 oz av = 20 p grains = 0.266 m
1 ounce avoirdupois (oz av)	= 28.3495 g = 141.75 cts = 567 p grains = 7.56 m
1 pearl grain (p grain)	= 0.05 g = 0.25 ct = 0.013 m = 0.0017 oz av
1 momme (m)	= 3.75 g = 18.75 cts = 75 p grains = 0.131 oz av

Length

When pricing pearls, you should take into consideration the length of the strand as well as the millimeter size of the pearls. The pearl trade has specific names for different necklace lengths. They are as follows:

1. Choker

A 14 to 16 inch (35 to 40 cm) necklace whose central pearl normally lies in the hollow of the throat or just below it. It looks especially attractive with V-neck blouses and dresses.

2. Princess

A 16 to 20 inch (40 to 50 cm) necklace. This slightly longer length is well suited for pearl enhancers (detachable pendants) and can slenderize the neck.

3. Matinee

A 20 to 26 inch (50 to 66 cm) necklace. Some people like to wear a matinee length along with a choker. Or they have it strung with two hidden (mystery) clasps so it can also be worn as a bracelet and shorter necklace.

4. Opera

A necklace about twice the size of a choker.

5. Rope

A necklace longer than an opera length. The defined length will vary according to the jeweler or company using the term.

Courtesy Mikimoto Co.

Pearl necklace lengths are summarized in the following list:

1.	Choker	14 - 16"	35 - 40 cm
2.	Princess	16 - 20"	40 - 50 cm
3.	Matinee	20 - 26"	50 - 66 cm
4.	Opera	28 - 36"	70 - 90 cm
5.	Rope	40" +	1 meter and longer

The above lengths are approximate. Definitions of necklace-length terms can vary from one jeweler to another. Keep in mind that pearl strands become slightly longer when knotted and strung with a clasp to form a necklace.

There are some other terms relating to pearl necklaces that consumers might not be familiar with. They are:

Bib

A necklace of 3 or more concentric strands. The lowest strand normally does not fall below a matinee length.

Dog collar

A multi-strand choker-length necklace. The strands may be clasped together in a single clasp. "Dog collars" help conceal neck wrinkles.

Torsade

A multi-strand necklace formed by twisting strands around each other. This is a popular way to wear freshwater pearl strands.

Uniform strand

A strand whose pearls are all about the same size.

Graduated strand

A strand with pearls of different sizes which gradually get larger towards the center. Graduated strands provide a big pearl look at a lower price than uniform strands.

Fig. 7.2 Dog-collar. Photo courtesy Cultured Pearl Associations of America & Japan.

81

8

Judging Make

Imagine spending fifteen years collecting over 30,000 pearls just to find the right pearls for one necklace. Someone in Texas took the trouble to do this. A picture of the resulting necklace can be seen in the fall 1990 issue of *Gems and Gemology* (page 224). The pearls on the strand have a variable fair to very good luster, most are round but some are off-round, they range in size from 3.70 mm to 8.15 mm, and their color ranges from brownish to purplish pink with a few pearls being pinkish orange.

This necklace could be classified as having an unusually fine make. Why? Because all of the pearls on the necklace were natural freshwater pearls recovered from lakes and rivers in West Texas. And it's amazing that so many pearls of this type could be so round and blend together so well. When judging make we have to take into account availability of the pearls being graded.

Make is a combination of the following factors:

♦ How well the pearls match or blend together in terms of color, shape, luster, size, and surface perfection
♦ How centered the drill holes are
♦ How smooth the size increase is of pearls in graduated strands

Some dealers charge a premium that may range from 1%-15% for Akoya strands that are of very fine make. Others may discount them if the pearls don't match very well. Premiums of up to 30% or more can be charged for well-matched pairs of large, high quality natural or South Sea pearls. It can take a lot of time and luck to find pearls that match.

Fine make is relative, though, and buyers should be flexible about their expectations. One should not expect South Sea, freshwater, or natural pearls of any kind to be as round and match as well as cultured Akoya pearls.

The definitions of what constitutes good, fair, and poor make in Akoya pearl strands can vary from one dealer to another. Some may emphasize color most. Uniform luster, size, and/or shape may be more important to other dealers, even though they would probably all agree that the overall appearance is what counts. An example of what dealers would agree is a poorly matched Akoya strand can be found in figure 8.1. The very-low-luster pearl brings down the grade considerably. The wide variation of color in this strand can be seen in color photo #2. Figure 8.2 is an example of a well-matched strand.

Fig. 8.1 Poorly matched strand

Fig. 8.2 Well-matched strand

There are questions that remain unanswered concerning the make of Akoya pearl strands:

♦ Should dyed and non-dyed Akoya strands be graded alike when it is a lot easier to match dyed pearls than those that aren't?

♦ Should a non-dyed pinkish strand be graded as strictly for make as a non-dyed cream-colored strand when cream colors are more plentiful?

♦ Should very-thick-nacre pearls be discounted as much for shape variations as thin- and medium-nacre pearls when pearls that are in the oyster longer have a greater chance of growing irregular?

We need to be careful not to become so concerned about perfect matching that we end up downplaying other quality factors. We also need to make sure that we are realistic about our expectations.

The author recalls being in Tokyo just after taking a pearl grading seminar. Somehow she had formed the idea that if the overtones of pearls in strands didn't match, they were unacceptable. She looked at some of the highest priced Akoya strands in some of most exclusive stores in Tokyo and was quite surprised to find not a single strand whose overtones matched. They all seemed to have a combination of green, pink, and silver overtones, but the strands varied in the percentage of each color. Finally, she realized that she was being unrealistic and that as long as the body color looked uniform and the overtones blended together well and their differences weren't obvious, there was nothing wrong with the pearls.

Judging make requires a balanced perspective. On the one hand, we shouldn't be so lax that we let shoddy workmanship become the norm. On the other, we shouldn't be so perfectionistic that no pearls can meet our standards. When you look at a strand of pearls consider its overall impact. Your attention should not be drawn away by obviously mismatched pearls. Neither is it desirable for the pearls to be lackluster but perfectly matched. Look at as many different qualities and strands of pearls as often as possible. You will form a sense of what's acceptable and eventually you'll have an appreciation for what is truly fine make.

9

South Sea Pearls

Mallory is puzzled. At the mall, she saw a large pearl ring in a jewelry store window for $4000. Then, in a another store window, she saw what appeared to be a ring of the same size and quality for $400. She went in and asked the salesman if it was a real pearl ring. He told her it was and suggested she try it on. She liked it, and considering the price of the other ring, felt she was getting a bargain, so she bought it. Now she is wondering why there was such a large difference in price between the two rings. Can you think of a possible explanation?

There is one. The pearl in the first ring was a whole **South Sea pearl**--a large whole pearl cultivated in a South Sea oyster. (In this chapter, "South Sea pearl" refers to white or light-colored pearls, not black ones). The pearl Mallory bought was a 3/4 mabe pearl--an assembled pearl, which was also probably from a South Sea oyster. A mabe pearl grows attached to the inner surface of the oyster shell. After it is cut from the shell, the nucleus bead which was inserted to make it grow is removed, and the remaining hole is filled with a paste or wax (and sometimes also a bead). Then it is covered with a mother-of-pearl backing. The resulting mabe pearl has a pearly nacre coating almost the same as a whole cultured pearl. The main difference is that it tends to be thinner. Consequently, some mabe pearls may crack very easily.

Even though the salesman was not wrong about the pearl being a real cultured one, he should have told Mallory it was an assembled pearl, especially since there is a vast price difference between mabe and whole pearls. But people don't always do what they're supposed to do. And some salespeople may not know the difference between a mabe pearl and a South Sea pearl (It should be noted that some people in the trade do not regard mabes as true pearls).

Mabe pearls are commonly shaped like half pearls, which makes them ideal for pendants and pins. They are also grown in 3/4 shapes to make them appear more like whole pearls when set in mountings such as rings. If a mabe pearl is loose, it's easy to tell it's assembled because the mother-of-pearl backing has a different appearance than the pearl nacre (fig 9.1). Plus you can see the line where the backing and pearl dome were glued together. When mounted, however, a mabe pearl may look like a South Sea pearl, particularly if the bottom of the pearl is encased in gold.

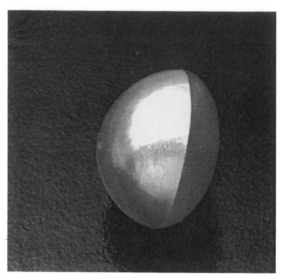

Fig. 9.1 Side view of a mabe pearl

Assembled pearls may occasionally be hard for professionals to detect. The winter 1989 issue of *Gems and Gemology* shows an assembled pearl which seemed to be a whole natural pearl when x-rayed (p. 240). But when it was unmounted, it became obvious that two pearl pieces had been glued together. The final GIA Gem Trade Laboratory report concluded "Assembled pearl consisting of two sections of natural pearl or blister pearls cemented together."

Large fine-quality whole pearls of any type are very rare and expensive. In April 1990, Sotheby's sold a strand of 45 cultured South Sea pearls ranging from 16 to 19 mm for $2,200,000. According to Sotheby's, the pearls were perfectly round and matched, and they had rose overtones and an exceptional luster.

South Sea pearls are cultivated in a variety of places--Australia, Burma (now called Myanmar), Thailand, Indonesia, the Philippines. The main source, however, has been Australia. In some seasons, it has produced up to 60% of the world's large South Sea pearls. (*National Geographic*, December 1991, p. 114 and *Pearls of the World*, p. 179). Australia's first pearl farm was established in 1956 on the Northwest coast at Kuri Bay. Prior to that time, Australia was producing up to 75% of the world's supply of mother of pearl, and pearls were just sold as a byproduct.

The silver-lip (Pinctada maxima) oyster is the main oyster used in Australia to cultivate South Sea pearls. If it's healthy, it can produce up to four pearls inserted at different times. The cultivation period may range from 1 1/2 to 2 years. The oysters that are unsuitable for whole pearls or that reject the bead nucleus are used to culture mabe pearls.

To avoid confusion, the pearl from the mabe oyster (Pteria penguin, penguin wing) has not been mentioned in this section. Some people regard it as the only true mabe pearl. However, it is not easy to find mabe-oyster pearls in areas such as North America. Most of the large mabe assembled pearls sold are cultivated in South Sea silver-lip or (sometimes) black-lip oysters and tend to have a lower luster and less iridescence than the mabe-oyster blister pearl. No matter where a mabe originates from, salespeople should never call them South Sea Pearls. Only a large whole pearl merits the price and name of "South Sea Pearl."

Judging Quality

South Sea pearls are judged according to their luster, color, shape, flaws, size, and nacre thickness as follows:

Luster

The higher the luster, the more valuable the pearl. White South Sea pearls have a lower luster potential than Akoya and black pearls. Take this into consideration when evaluating white pearls. For tips on how to judge luster, see Chapter 4.

Color

As is the case with Akoya pearls, choice of color should be based on what will look best on the person who will wear the pearls. The color varies depending on which variety of Pinctada maxima oyster the pearl comes from--the silver-lip or gold-lip. The silver-lip oyster, the main oyster in Australia, tends to produce silvery white pearls. The gold-lip variety, which is more commonly found around countries such as Indonesia, Thailand, and the Philippines, is more likely to produce golden or cream-colored pearls.

The color of South Sea pearls is judged in about the same way as it is in Akoya pearls. White and pink pearls are more highly valued than yellowish pearls. The presence of pink overtones and iridescence is very desirable.

In the past, Burmese pearls were prized for their fine color, largely because of their pink overtones. Pearls from Australia, which were less valued, tended to be white with no pink overtones. Burmese pearls no longer have the same prestige. Recently there was a pearl auction in Burma. One dealer describes the pearls there as "mostly reject quality." This decline started after the departure of Japanese technicians and cultivators.

The quality of Australian pearls, however, has improved, especially their color. Now instead of being greenish or just white, many of their pearls have pink overtones. Consequently, high-quality pearls from Australia now have the prestige that once was accorded to those from Burma.

Shape

The more round the pearl the more valuable it is. But round South Sea pearls are very rare, far more rare than Akoya pearls, which are smaller and have thinner nacre. Normally the shape of South Sea pearls ranges from off-round to baroque, with baroque being the most common and least expensive.

Be willing to compromise on shape. This may be necessary due to the high price and limited availability of round South Sea pearls.

Flaws

South Sea pearls are graded for flaws in the same way as Akoya pearls, except with much more leniency. The fewer the flaws the higher the price.

Size

South Sea pearls generally range in size from 10 to 18 mm. The world's largest round South Sea pearl may be 20.8 mm (over 3/4"). A picture of it is in the December 1991 issue of *National Geographic* (p. 115). Baroque pearls can grow larger. The "Nugget of Australia," a pearl belonging to the collection of Golay Buchel, has a length of 25 mm and weighs 90.6 ct. (*Pearls of the World* p. 116). It's their large size that makes South Sea pearls so expensive. As would be expected, the larger the pearl the greater its value.

The size of a cultured pearl is primarily determined by the size of its bead nucleus. The bigger the oyster, the bigger bead it can accept and the bigger pearl it can grow. Consequently, small Japanese oysters which measure 4 inches (10 mm) across, produce smaller pearls than the silver or gold-lip oysters which can measure 12 inches (30 mm) across. Black-pearl oysters, which also produce white pearls grow up to about 8 inches (20 mm) across and produce a pearl in between the size of the silver- and gold-lip oysters.

Nacre Thickness

Big pearls do not necessarily have thick nacre. As with Akoya pearls, the nacre thickness of cultured South Sea pearls has decreased during the past 30 years. In the April 1971 issue of *Lapidary Journal*, Australian pearl farmer C. Denis George stated that a good cultured South Sea pearl had a nacre thickness double the radius of the bead nucleus. In other words, a 15-mm pearl had about a 5-mm nacre thickness and a nucleus whose radius is about 2.5 mm. If this standard were used today, it would be very hard to find a good South Sea pearl. Judging from standards published by black pearl producers, South Sea pearls today should have a nacre thickness of at least 1 mm of the radius. (See nacre thickness section in Chapter 10).

Fig. 9.2 Tahitian black pearl necklace (15.3 to 12 mm) and a South Sea pearl necklace with Australian and Burmese pearls ranging from 14.8 to 11.8 mm. Photo courtesy Albert Asher South Sea Pearl Co.

One millimeter may sound thick compared to the minimum standard this book suggests for Akoya pearls--0.35 mm. Keep in mind, though, that Akoya pearls have a finer-grained nacre than South Sea pearls and they are smaller. A 0.5-mm thickness on a 6-mm Akoya pearl is 1/6 of the radius. A 1-mm thickness on a 12-mm South Sea pearl is also 1/6 of the radius. Therefore, it is reasonable for buyers to expect nacre at least 1 mm thick on their South Sea pearls, especially considering their high cost.

Thin nacre is not as easily detected in South Sea pearls as it is in Akoya pearls. Due to the thicker nacre, the shell layers of the bead do not show up as well and it's harder to see the bead nucleus through the drill hole. In addition, the pearls are often mounted in jewelry so the drill holes are not visible.

To avoid buying South Sea pearls with nacre that's too thin, consumers should select pearls with a good luster and deal with jewelers who consider nacre thickness important. Also they should have their pearls x-rayed by a gem lab when the price of the pearls is high enough to warrant the cost of an x-ray report, which is about $100 to $300. The nacre thickness can be measured in the x-ray photograph.

Like all other pearls, those from the South Seas come in a wide range of qualities and prices. Some sell for over $30,000 and some sell for $100. The price factors above are what determine the value. For example, just take a $30,000 dollar South Sea pearl, make it smaller, add lots of flaws, give it a baroque shape, color it yellow, and give it a dull drab luster. What can be the result? A $100 South Sea pearl.

Quiz (Chapters 7, 8 and 9)

Select the Correct Answer

1. Which would be the hardest to match?

a. Dyed Akoya pearls with very thick nacre
b. Dyed Akoya pearls with thin nacre
c. Non-dyed Akoya pearls with very thick nacre
d. Non-dyed Akoya pearls with thin nacre

2. Which would be the easiest to match?

a. 9 to 9 1/2 mm Akoya pearls
b. 9 to 9 1/2 mm South Sea pearls
c. 6 to 6 1/2 mm Akoya pearls
d. A graduated strand of South Sea pearls

3. Which of the following necklace lengths is shortest?

a. Opera
b. Matinee
c. Princess
d. Rope

4. Larger pearls can be cultivated in the South Seas than in Japan because:

a. the oysters in the South Seas are exposed to more sunlight.
b. South Sea oysters are larger than the Japanese Akoya type.
c. there are so many tropical fish for South Sea oysters to feed on.
d. none of the above

5. Which country has produced the most South Sea pearls and mother of pearl?

a. Burma
b. Australia
c. Japan
d. The Philippines

6. Which of these units of weight is heaviest?

a. 1 carat
b. 1 gram
c. 1 ounce avoirdupois
d. 1 pearl grain
e. 1 momme

7. Which of the following weighs the least?

a. 1 carat
b. 1 gram
c. 1 ounce avoirdupois
d. 1 pearl grain
e. 1 momme

True or False?

8. It's easier to match natural pearls than cultured pearls.

9. Mabe assembled pearls cost a lot less than South Sea pearls.

10. There's a regular rise in price as pearl size increases.

11. Two matched pearls can cost a lot more than two unmatched ones.

12. Since South Sea pearls are so big, there's no need to be concerned about the thickness of their nacre.

13. The effect of size on price can vary from one dealer to another.

Answers:

1. c

2. c

3. c

4. b

5. b

6. c

7. d

8. F   It's a lot harder to match natural pearls.

9. T

10. F   Price jumps tend to be uneven.

11. T

12. F

13. T

10

Black Pearls

Gray. Is this an appealing color for a gem? For a diamond, it wouldn't be, nor would it be for a sapphire. But judging from the prices of "black pearls," pearl connoisseurs find dark gray very appealing. In April 1990, for example, a single strand of 27 black pearls was sold for $880,000 at Sotheby's. This was more than $32,000 per pearl.

Black pearls are not necessarily black. More often than not they range from a medium to very dark gray. Also the colors of pearls that look black may be natural or dyed.

If you go to Hong Kong, for example, you may see strands labeled "black pearls" that sell for a few hundred dollars. They are probably artificially colored Akoya pearls whose natural color was undesirable. In Tahiti, **"black pearl"** can only refer to **a dark-colored pearl of natural color from the black-lip oyster** (Pinctada margaritifera). The jewelers in both areas are correct in their use of the term. In both cases the pearls are dark-colored and they are real cultured pearls. This book, however, uses the Tahitian meaning of "black pearl" because that is the one accepted by the major wholesalers of fine-quality pearls.

Naturally-colored black pearls can also be confused with naturally-colored "blue pearls." Unlike black pearls whose color is an inherent characteristic of the pearl nacre, **blue pearls** derive their color from foreign contaminants in the nacre itself or between the nacre and the shell bead nucleus. Naturally-colored, dark Akoya pearls are good examples of "blue pearls." They may be blue, black, gray, or brown. Black pearls and "blue pearls" can look the same but due to the difference in the origin of their color, "blue pearls" are worth less. The fact that "blue pearls" might decay or lose their color if holes are drilled through them is another reason for their lower value. (A more detailed analysis of black pearls and "blue pearls" is given by Yoshihiro Hisada and Hiroshi Komatsu of the Mikimoto Co. in *Pearls of the World* (pp. 87-94) and Hiroshi Komatsu and Shigeru Akamatsu in the Spring 78 issue of *Gems & Gemology* (pp. 7-15)).

Since there can be a great value difference between black pearls, "blue pearls" and artificially colored pearls even though they may look the same, consumers need to be concerned about buying black pearls that are misrepresented. Later in the chapter, some guidelines are given on how to spot pearls that are not really black pearls. Keep in mind, though, that the only sure way to identify a black pearl is to send it to a lab and have it tested.

Fig. 10.1 An array of white and black pearls from the South Seas. The white necklace is Burmese and the black ones Tahitian. The largest pearl in the oyster shell measures 18.2 mm and is from Burma. Photo courtesy Albert Asher South Sea Pearl Co.

It's only been within the last 10 to 20 years that cultured black pearls have become commercially important. Most of them are cultivated in Tahiti (French Polynesia to be more accurate) and others are produced in places like Okinawa and Fiji. Natural black pearls, however, became known in Europe after Hernando Cortez and later explorers discovered colored pearls in the Gulf of California. In the late 1700's and early 1800's, La Paz in Baja California became the black pearl center of the world. Natural black pearls in the South Seas were also being fished at this time. Gradually black pearls grew popular especially among European royalty, such as Empress Eugenie of France. But the oyster beds were overfished and black pearls became scarce. Then in the 1940's, a large percentage of the black lip oysters in the Gulf of California died for unknown reasons. Today, even though natural pearls are occasionally found, you should assume that unless otherwise specified, the black pearls sold in stores are cultured. Because of this, throughout the rest of this chapter the term "black pearl" will refer to cultured dark pearls of natural color found in the black-lip oyster.

Judging Quality

A black pearl is judged according to its luster, color, shape, flaws, size, and nacre thickness as follows:

Luster

Black pearls can look almost metallic. You should expect a higher and different luster from them than you would from white South Sea pearls. Dark nacre does not reflect light in the same way that white nacre does. The best way to learn the luster potential of a black pearl is to look at some black pearls ranging from very low to very high in luster. After you compare them, you probably won't be satisfied with a black pearl of low luster. Keep in mind that lighting can affect black pearls in the same way it does white pearls, so compare pearls under equivalent lighting conditions. (See Chapter 4 for discussion of lighting.)

Low luster in black pearls is often correlated with thin nacre, as is the case with white pearls. But thin-nacre black pearls can have good luster and thick-nacre pearls may have low luster. Consequently, it's best to treat luster and nacre thickness as two separate value factors.

Color

Generally the darker the black pearl, the more valuable it is. The finest black pearls also have a green overtone which is called "peacock green. A solid black pearl with no overtone is considered undesirable and may cost as much as 50% less than one of similar quality with green overtones. Pearls with muddy colors are also viewed as undesirable.

Other overtone colors on black pearls are pink, blue, gold, silver, and a reddish purple called "aubergine," which is the French word for eggplant. These overtones may be present in a variety of combinations and are considered a plus factor. Black pearls also have a wide range of body colors--black, gray, blue, green, brown.

There is no standardized system throughout the pearl industry for classifying or valuing the color of black pearls, and considering the complexity of it, there may never be. There is no standard either for determining how dark a pearl must be to be called "black" (black-lip oysters produce pearls ranging in color from white to gray to black). There is, however, general agreement that the most valued color for a black pearl is an evenly distributed greenish black which may or may not have reddish-purple highlights. This is a contrast from Akoya pearls where greenish tints are not highly valued.

Shape

Round shapes are the most expensive. The more perfectly round the pearl, the more valued it is. Pear and drop shapes are the next most expensive. The more symmetrical these shapes are, the more their value. Baroque shapes and circled pearls with ring-like formations around them are the least expensive (figs. 10.2 and 10.3).

Fig. 10.2 Baroque-shape Tahitian black pearl

Fig. 10.3 Circled black pearl

When you need to cut down on the price of a black pearl, shape is a good category to compromise on. In fact, baroque and circled pearls often make more interesting jewelry pieces than round pearls do.

Size

Naturally the bigger the black pearl the more expensive it is. Black pearls generally range in size from about 9 to 18 mm with their average size tending to be between 9 and 11.5

mm. Some baroque black pearls may reach 25 to 30 mm. Size has a great impact on price. A 1 mm increase in the size of medium-quality pearls can raise their price 100 to 200%. In other words, a 14 mm pearl which costs $5,000, might cost $10,000 if it were 15 mm and $30,000 if it were 16 mm.

At the retail level black pearls tend to be described and priced according to millimeter size. Weight may be used as an additional means of identifying them. This is the opposite of round diamonds where the price is based on the weight, but measurements may be given to help distinguish them from other diamonds of the same weight.

On the wholesale level, however, large lots of black pearls are sold according to their weight, which is measured in momme (1 momme = 3.75 grams = 18.75 carats). The pearls are graded into various categories, and each category is assigned a per-momme price.

Fig. 10.4 Tahitian black pearl necklace, natural color. The baroque pearl in the pendant measures 18 x 13 mm. Photo courtesy Albert Asher South Sea Pearl Co.

Flaws

Flaws can decrease the price of black pearls considerably, which is an advantage for consumers. A black pearl can often be mounted in a way that will hide its flaws when worn. This means if you select your pearl(s) carefully, you can have a clean-looking one for a lower price. Remember that blemishes on single pearls tend to be more obvious than on those in strands. Therefore, when buying a loose black pearl, figure out in advance how you will wear it so you can choose one whose flaws won't be noticeable.

Nacre thickness

It should be at least 1 mm (of the radius). The thicker the nacre the more valuable the pearl.

As you are shopping, you may encounter salespeople who claim that all black or white pearls from the South Seas have thick nacre, and that nacre thickness need not be a consideration. Many people who specialize in producing or studying black pearls would disagree.

Dr. Jean-Paul Lintilhac, installer and developer of two black pearl farms in Tahiti, is one example. In his book, *Black Pearls of Tahiti*, he states that jewelers in Tahiti are worried about the thinness of the nacre of some of the pearls offered to them for sale. He goes on to say that certain pearl farmers are in such a hurry to recover their investment that they harvest their pearls prematurely and as a result the nacre is very thin. Then he writes (p. 85):

> "Formerly a big pearl meant a good thickness of nacre, but with the supergrafts used today, size is no guarantee. If you are buying a big expensive pearl, you have the right to ask for an x-ray of it which will enable you to see and measure the thickness of the layers of nacre surrounding the nucleus. One millimeter of nacre is a minimum for a good pearl."

Tahiti Pearls, a major black pearl company, also tells consumers in their book *The Magic of the Black Pearl*, that nacre thickness is a criteria used to judge black pearls. They indicate a 1 mm to 1.5 mm nacre thickness as an appropriate range for black pearls.

Hisada and Komatsu of the Mikimoto Co. put nacre thickness at the top of their list of black pearl quality factors (*Pearls of the World* p. 90). They state:

> "Nacre thickness is a basic factor in judging the elegance of the pearl. Its beauty and durability depend on the thickness of the nacre, its quality and quantity."

The Mikimoto company, in their leaflet "The Art of Selecting Cultured Pearls," tells consumers: "For beautiful pearls the most important factors are luster and nacre thickness."

Chapter 4 gives guidelines on determining if the nacre thickness of Akoya pearls is acceptable. Unfortunately these techniques do not work as well on black pearls. It's often impossible to see into their drill holes because the pearls may be glued to a jewelry piece such as a ring or pendant mounting. Also the nacre of black pearls may mask the layers of a shell bead nucleus that might be visible in a thin-nacre Akoya pearl.

Usually the best way of determining the nacre thickness of a black pearl is with an x-ray. And, if you are spending thousands of dollars on a pearl piece, it's well worth your money to have a gem lab x-ray the piece to check for nacre thickness and to determine if the color is natural. But what should you do if you are paying, say $500 for a black pearl pendant? An x-ray in a case like this is probably not worth the money. The best thing you can do is to choose pearls with as high of a luster as possible and **buy your pearls from jewelers who consider nacre thickness important.** If they don't think it's important and they don't mention it, this might either mean they have something to hide or they don't take it into consideration when buying pearls for their inventory. And as a consequence, their pearls may not have an adequate nacre thickness.

It's often hard to understand why one pearl may cost $50 and another may cost $1000. But let's consider how the above factors might work together to lower the price. If a pearl costing $1000 decreases 1 mm in size, it's price may drop 50% to $500. If it then changes from a dark greenish grey color to a muddy gray with no overtones, it's price could drop another 50% to $250. Going from a very high to very low luster could bring its price to $125. And then adding lots of flaws to it could bring it down to $50.

Pearl pricing is not as mathematically regular as this example. Nevertheless, the above quality factors can have a similar effect on its price. So take them into consideration as you shop and compare prices. Also, when you look at pearl prices in ads and catalogues, remember that they are meaningless if an adequate description of the pearls is not included.

Natural Color or Not?

Off-color pearls from the Akoya and silver- or gold-lip oysters are sometimes blackened to improve their appearance. Light-colored pearls from the black-lip oyster are occasionally darkened because the lighter colors of this oyster tend to be less valued. The following methods are used to darken pearls.

♦ **Silver salt treatment:** This is the most common way of blackening Akoya pearls. The pearls are soaked in a weak solution of silver nitrate and dilute ammonia and then exposed to light or hydrogen sulfide gas.

♦ **Irradiation:** This method works best on freshwater pearls, but occasionally off-color Akoya pearls are darkened in this manner. It involves bombarding pearls with gamma rays. This blackens the shell bead nucleus of Akoya pearls and makes their nacre appear dark. .

♦ **Dying the bead nucleus:** Occasionally the shell bead nuclei are dyed before they are inserted in the oyster. Afterwards the dark bead shows through the nacre and makes the pearl nacre look dark.

♦ **Plastic coating**: In a few instances, pearls have been darkened with thin plastic coatings. This coating can be easily detected by its strange feel and by bald spots on the pearl where the coating may have worn away.

According to the GIA pearl grading course, the color of irradiated pearls and those colored with silver salts is stable. People who deal in dyed black pearls also state that pearls treated with these two methods do not fade. Occasionally, though, there are reports of dyed black pearls that lose their color. Perhaps this is because the bead nucleus was dyed instead of irradiated or because the irradiation or silver nitrate treatments were done improperly. For your protection, buy dyed pearls from reputable jewelers. That way if there is a problem, you'll be able to return the pearls and get a refund.

As one can see, dyeing is not the only means of coloring pearls. Nevertheless, for the sake of brevity, the term "**dyed**" will be used in the rest of this chapter to describe any artificially colored pearl.

Many people associate the term "dyed" with the terms "cheap" and "fake." However, dyed black pearls were sold in fashionable stores as far back as the 1930's--long before black pearls were being commercially cultivated. Dyed black pearls were considered elegant. They are still in demand. Plus they have the added bonus of being much more affordable than their naturally-colored counterparts. A large percentage of the pink pearls sold in stores have also been dyed and this means there's a wider selection of pink pearls available for consumers. The only thing wrong with dyeing pearls is denying it is done and not disclosing it to buyers.

Dyed pearls are not fakes, but they are normally considered less valuable than those of natural color. There is an especially large price difference between true black pearls and those that aren't, so you need to know how to protect yourself from being charged a black pearl price for a dyed pearl. Even if the price is fair, you may just want to avoid buying a dyed black pearl. You can reduce your chances of being misled with the following tests:

Price Test   Is the price unusually low compared to true black pearls of the same size, shape, and overall quality? An average-quality, round, 8-mm Tahitian black pearl can retail for between $300 to $500. A round, 8-mm dyed black pearl may retail for about $50 to $100. Higher qualities will cost more. (Remember to compare pearls of the same size and shape. These factors have a major effect on the price. For example, if we just decreased the size of the dyed black pearl to 6 mm, it could retail for about $15.)

True black pearls are typically expensive, so if the price is low and you are not in Tahiti, assume the pearl is dyed unless otherwise told. (It's illegal to import or sell dyed black pearls in Tahiti.) If the store claims the color is natural, ask if they will write this on the receipt.

Size Test

Is the size less than 9 mm? If so and you are not in Tahiti, assume that it is an Akoya dyed pearl or "blue pearl" unless the store is willing to write on the receipt that it is naturally colored and from the black lip oyster. There are true black pearls less than 9 mm, but it is usually not cost effective to intentionally produce them when farmers can get far more by cultivating larger pearls. Keep in mind, too, that black pearls below 9 mm may be small due to thin nacre.

Akoya oysters, on the other hand, can produce a wide range of pearls below 9 mm ; but rarely do they grow round pearls above 10 mm. Larger Japanese baroque pearls may be available. A photo of some Japanese "blue pearls" ranging from 11.5 to 14 mm can be seen in the fall 1990 issue of *Gems & Gemology* (p. 225).

Once in a while, large round pearls from South Sea oysters are dyed or are "blue pearls." Therefore large size is never proof that a pearl is a true black pearl. It is, however, a positive sign. When buying black pearls, it's always advisable to ask salespeople to specify on the receipt that the pearls are of natural color and from the black lip oyster. When spending large sums of money, also have them tested by an independent gem lab.

Color Test

Are the pearls so dark they are almost black? Do all the pearls in the piece look the exact same color? Is the color perfectly even in all the pearls? These are indications the pearls might be dyed. It's not easy to find true black pearls that are really black. More often than not they are grayish. It's also not easy to find several black pearls the exact same even color.

If you are interested in black pearls, look at a lot of them. Then look at dyed pearls and compare. Gradually, you will get a sense of what the body colors and overtones of black pearls look like. People that work with black pearls on a regular basis can usually spot dyed pearls instantly. But even experts can be fooled. So when making a major purchase, have your black pearls tested by an independent gem lab.

Shape Test

Are the pearls perfectly round? This is a sign they might be dyed, especially if the price is reasonable. Do they have ring-like formations encircling them? This is a characteristic of Tahitian black pearls. Perfectly round black pearls are rare, which is one reason they are so expensive. Tahitian black pearls often have distinctive shapes and slightly uneven surfaces (figs. 10.2 & 10.3).

Drill-hole Test

If it is possible to look into the drill hole with a loupe, does the nacre inside look white and the nucleus look dark? This is a sign the pearl has been colored by irradiation or the nucleus has been dyed. Is there dye concentrated around the drill hole? This indicates it is dyed.

Infrared Photo Test

If you have a camera, you can photograph the pearls with color infrared film (Kodak, Ektachrome Infrared Film, IE 135-20). Naturally colored pearls tend to look blue, whereas pearls colored with silver salts generally look yellow (or range from greenish blue to yellow green). (Komatsu and Akamatsu, *Gems & Gemology*, Spring 1978). You can use the leftover film to take some interesting aerial photographs. This film is used for topographical analysis.

The following methods require special equipment, but you might be interested in tests that labs may conduct:

UV Fluorescence Test

The pearls are examined under long-wave UV radiation. Natural-color black pearls will generally have a fluorescence ranging from a bright red (pearls from Baja California) to a dull reddish brown (Tahitian pearls). Dyed pearls tend to show no reaction or else fluoresce a dull green. (See page 143 of the 1989 issue of *Gems & Gemology*, part of a good article on the Polynesian black pearl by Marisa Goebel and Dona Dirlam.)

High Magnification

The pearls are viewed under 100+-power magnification through crossed polaroid lenses. Traces of the chemical coloring can be seen. (Hisada and Komatsu, *Pearls of the World*, pp. 92-93).

X-radiograph Test

An x-ray photo called an **x-radiograph** is taken of the pearls. If the pearls are dyed with silver salts, a pale ring between the nacre and the shell bead nucleus can often be seen. Plus there is less of a contrast between the bead and the nacre.

X-ray Fluorescence Test The pearls are exposed to x-rays. Then the emitted wavelengths are measured with an instrument called a spectrometer to detect trace elements such as silver on the surface of the pearl.

As you can see, there is a wide variety of tests for identifying black pearls. Use a combination of the simple tests to help you spot obvious cases of dye. But when it comes to making a major purchase, get help from professionals.

Chapter 10 Quiz

Select the Correct Answer

1. The most valued black pearls have

a. no overtones
b. green overtones
c. silver overtones
d. pink overtones

2. Which of the following is not used to darken the color of pearls?

a. Irradiation
b. Silver salt treatment
c. Heat treatment
d. Colored dyes

3. The size of most natural-color black pearls is usually:

a. less than 9 mm.
b. between 9 and 12 mm
c. between 11 and 15 mm
d. greater than 11.5 mm

4. A dyed-black pearl may have originally been:

a. an off-color Akoya pearl.
b. a light-color pearl from a black-lip oyster.
c. an off-color pearl from an Australian silver-lip oyster.
d. any of the above.

5. Which of the following shapes is the least expensive for a black pearl?

a. round
b. pear-shape
c. circled
d. oval

6. Today most natural-color black pearls are cultivated in:

a. Japan
b. Baja California
c. French Polynesia (Tahiti)
d. Australia

7. The term "black pearl" is used by jewelry salespeople to refer to:

a. natural-color black pearls from the black-lip oyster
b. "blue pearls"
c. dyed black pearls
d. all of the above

True or False?

8. Most black pearls are very round.

9. Gray pearls are not considered to be black pearls.

10. Some cultured black pearls have an inadequate nacre coating.

11. If a pearl is black and over 11 mm in size, its color is natural.

12. Ring-like formation are often seen on Tahitian black pearls.

13. The most reliable way of determining if the color of a black pearl is natural is to have it x-rayed by a gem lab.

14. The color of "blue pearls" is stable.

15. There is no standard for determining how dark a pearl must be to be called black.

Answers:

1. b

2. c

3. b

4. d   But if it's less than 8.5 mm, it was probably an off-color Akoya pearl.

5. c

6. c

7. d   Even though this chapter uses the term "black pearl" to refer to natural-color pearls from the black-lip oyster, you should be aware that some people in the trade also use it to refer to any dark colored pearl, even "blue pearls" and dyed pearls. Therefore, always ask salespeople to specify what they mean by "black pearl."

8. F

9. F

10. T

11. F   Large pearls from the black-lip and silver-lip oysters are also dyed.

12. T

13. T

14. F   Due to their organic pigmentation, "blue pearls" can lose color or decay if holes are drilled through them. (See page 22 of *Pearls* by Shohei Shirai and the other references cited in the first section of this chapter.)

15. T

11

Freshwater Pearls

Bob is in Hong Kong and he's looking at some strands of little pearls that resemble rice. They're white, they glisten, and they are just $5. Since the price is so low, Bob thinks they might be fake. Is he probably right?

No, he's probably wrong. Even though there are imitation pearls like this, it's more likely that they are cultured Chinese freshwater pearls (also called sweetwater pearls). These "Rice-Krispie-like" pearls are usually inexpensive because as many as 50 of them may be found in one mussel, they don't take long to grow (often just 12 months), they can be harvested two or three times from the same mussel unlike Akoya pearls, and Chinese labor costs are low.

The term "Chinese rice pearl" often has negative connotations because so many cheap, poor-quality ones have been produced. There are two main reasons for this low quality: Chinese pearl cultivators tend to be less skilled than those in Japan, and Chinese mussels are often overcrowded in the lakes and ponds and thereby deprived of essential nutrients. The Chinese also produce some high-quality pearls. The best ones come from the Sankakugai or Triangle-shaped oyster, a different mollusk than the one used for rice pearls. High-quality rice pearls are also available.

Even though freshwater pearls in the shape of Buddha had been cultured in China as far back as the thirteenth century, the Japanese, at Lake Biwa, are credited with being the first to succeed in cultivating freshwater pearls on a commercial basis. The technical roots of cultivating freshwater pearls are attributed to Masayo Fujita, the "Father of Freshwater Pearl Cultivation" (p. 136, *Pearls of the World*, article by Hidemi Takashima, a chief engineer at the Nippon Institute for Scientific Rescarch on Pearls).

The first harvest of Biwa pearls was in August 1925 and they had a shell bead nucleus like Akoya oysters. By the 1930's they were being sold overseas. Some merchants from India would buy these Lake Biwa pearls from Fujita and then resell them to the Middle East as highly valuable Persian pearls for huge sums of money. One day, it was accidentally discovered that a shell bead is not necessary for the cultivation of a freshwater pearl. All that is needed is the insertion of a piece of mantle (a membranous tissue that secretes nacre and lines the inner shell surface of mollusks). This is a lot less trouble than inserting both a bead and mantle tissue. Also, it was noticed that after the first harvest, mussels can spontaneously grow pearls a second and third time. What this now means is that cultured freshwater pearls usually have more pearl nacre than cultured Akoya pearls because most do not have a shell bead nucleus.

China and Japan are not the only places where freshwater pearls are found. There are many historical accounts about the natural freshwater pearls of Europe and North America. These pearls are still being sold (primarily at gem shows), but in decreasing quantities. Overfishing and pollution has either dwindled or, in some areas, eliminated the supply of these natural pearls.

The cultured freshwater pearl market in the United States, however, is gradually increasing. They are now being cultivated in Tennessee. This area is also known for being the primary source of the shell beads in Akoya pearls. David Federman reports in the September 1991 issue of *Modern Jeweler* that the Marysville area in California is also slated to become a producer of freshwater cultured pearls. This means that a wider selection of pearls could be available for consumers. The next section describes how these pearls may differ in quality.

Judging Quality

The grading of freshwater pearls is more variable than that of saltwater pearls. Nevertheless, there is agreement about certain value factors. Freshwater pearls are generally valued according to the following criteria:

Luster

The higher and more even the luster, the greater the value. Low-quality freshwater pearls may seem lustrous to a layperson because often part of their surface is very shiny. However, if some areas of the pearls look milky, chalky, and dull, they are considered to have a low luster. In high-quality freshwater pearls, there is an evenly distributed luster and a high contrast between the light and dark areas of the pearls.

When judging freshwater pearls for luster, examine them on a white background under a bare direct light and be sure to roll them so you can see their entire surface area. If possible, compare strands of different qualities. It's important that your eye become sensitive to luster variations because luster is one of the most important determinants of value in pearls of all types.

Smoothness

The smoother the pearl, the more valuable it is. Even though bumpy, wrinkled surfaces can lower the value of freshwater pearls, the bumps and wrinkles are not considered flaws. Consequently, this chapter treats smoothness as a separate category from blemish.

Figures 11.1 and 11.2 can help you understand how the luster and smoothness of freshwater pearls can affect their value. Both strands are Chinese rice pearls. The lower one retails for $16 in a 32" strand (the pearls average 4 to 5 mm--3/8 inch in length). The upper one with larger pearls could retail for about $2. The reason for this price difference is that the lower strand is a lot smoother and has a much better luster than the $2 strand.

Fig. 11.1 Upper strand--poor quality "rice" pearls, lower strand--good quality "rice" pearls. Compare their smoothness and the evenness of their luster. (3X)

Fig. 11.2 Enlarged view of same strands (7X mag.)

The price difference becomes more noticeable when several strands are twisted to form one necklace. For example, a ten-strand twist of the higher quality pearls would retail for maybe $160 plus the cost of the clasp. Whereas the lower-quality one might be just $20.

Size/Weight

Size is a very important price factor for freshwater pearls. One of the main reasons the high-quality strand of rice pearls in figure 11.1 retails for only $16 is because the pearls are so small. For the most part, the largest cultured freshwater pearls have come from Japan.

Freshwater pearls prices are generally quoted by weight or by the strand. The gram is probably the most common unit of weight used at the retail level, but some dealers quote prices according to carat weight. Suppliers of large quantities of pearls may use the "momme" which equals 3.75 grams or 18.75 carats. The measurements of pearls are often listed along with their weight as an additional description and means of identification. The size of round freshwater pearls may be expressed by their diameter, measured in millimeters.

Shape

Usually the more round a pearl is, the greater its value. Most freshwater pearls have baroque shapes. The fatter shapes may be priced higher than ovalish or thin ones. It's been suggested this might be due to their thicker nacre coating.

Specific types of baroque shapes sometimes command higher prices. For example, one dealer has found that the cross is the most expensive shape for cultured freshwater pearls that have no shell nucleus. Good symmetry can also make a shape more valuable.

Pearl shapes are determined by a variety of factors:

♦ The type of irritant causing the pearl--mantle tissue, shell bead plus mantle tissue, or in the case of natural pearls parasite or shell piece. Round pearls are more easily cultivated with shell beads. Most freshwater pearl mussels are implanted only with mantle tissue.

♦ The shape of the irritant. Pearl shapes tend to conform to that of the irritant. It's relatively easy to cut mantle tissue in a variety of shapes. This is one of the main reasons freshwater pearls come in so many different shapes which make them ideal for creative jewelry designs.

♦ The length of the cultivation period. Generally the longer the pearl is in the oyster, the more likely it is to have an irregular shape. With Chinese rice pearls, though, too short of a cultivation period may increase their chances of looking wrinkled and unsymmetrical.

♦ The position of the irritant in the mollusk. If the pearl is in a spot where it can be turned as the mollusk moves around, it may have a greater chance of growing smoothly and symmetrically.

♦ The quality of the irritant. For example, baroque shapes are sometimes the result of flaws in the shell bead nuclei.

Flaws

Obvious flaws such as discolorations, pits, cavities, and rough spots can decrease the value of a pearl considerably, especially if the pearl is otherwise of high quality. Normally, though, flaws in freshwater pearls are not very noticeable, due to their baroque shapes. Consequently, flaws tend to have less of an effect on the value of freshwater pearls than on those of saltwater origin. However, if a single freshwater pearl has a large flaw like the one in figure 11.4, this can lower its price significantly.

Fig. 11.3 Discoloration & hole on a Chinese "rice" pearl. (9X)

Fig. 11.4 Cavity on an American freshwater pearl. The shell nucleus is about to show through. (3.5X)

Color

Freshwater pearls come in a wide variety of body colors--white, pink, orange, yellow, lavender, gray, bronze. Some pearls are even bi-colored. When you ask freshwater pearl dealers what are the most valued body colors, you get a variety of answers. Some of their responses are:

♦ Pink.
♦ White, because that is what's most in demand.
♦ Mauve and metallic.
♦ Colored pearls, due to their rarity, are much more valuable than white pearls.
♦ It doesn't matter what the color is as long as it is not dull and dingy.
♦ Naturally-colored pearls of any color are the most valuable because they are not bleached and processed like white pearls.
♦ Naturally-colored pearls, and the more intense their color, the greater their value. Perhaps true bronze pearls would cost the most because they are so hard to find.

♦ "We price the colors all about the same. Except we add a 5% premium to mauve-colored pearls if they are of high quality because there's a large demand for them in America. We discount our cream-colored freshwater pearls from about 1% to 5%."

What these answers indicate is that the color grading of freshwater pearls is very flexible. Therefore, the best way to know how an individual pearl dealer prices color is to ask.

Most freshwater pearl dealers agree on the following:

♦ The body color does not affect the price of freshwater pearls as much as it does that of saltwater pearls.

♦ The presence of overtone colors such as pink, silver, and blue makes them more valuable. This is because pearls with high luster have overtone colors. On the other hand, a soapy-looking, solid-white color is typical of pearls with a very low luster.

♦ Iridescence (orient) increases the value of pearls. Iridescence and high luster are also interrelated.

Nacre thickness and type of nucleus

Nacre thickness is not as important of a factor in cultured freshwater pearls as it is in saltwater pearls. This is because most freshwater pearls do not have a shell nucleus. When one is present, the nacre tends to be thicker. One of the biggest selling points of freshwater pearls is that they usually have a higher percentage of pearl nacre than their saltwater counterparts.

Cultured freshwater pearls with a shell nucleus often command premium prices. This is because the shell nucleus helps create a pearl which is larger and more regular in shape than one cultured only with mantle tissue.

Place of Origin, Price Factor or Not?

Some members of the pearl industry state that the value of a pearl is based on its quality and size, not on where it comes from. Others feel that the source of a pearl **can** have an impact on its value. Two examples are:

♦ Japanese Biwa pearls tend to be more highly valued than freshwater pearls cultured in other countries.

♦ Saltwater pearls tend to sell for more than freshwater pearls.

We can get a clearer perspective of the gem origin controversy by examining how origin affects the price of other products such as wine. California and France both produce high-quality wines. Yet because France has a longer history of fine wine making, top-quality French wines tend to cost more and enjoy a greater prestige than those from California.

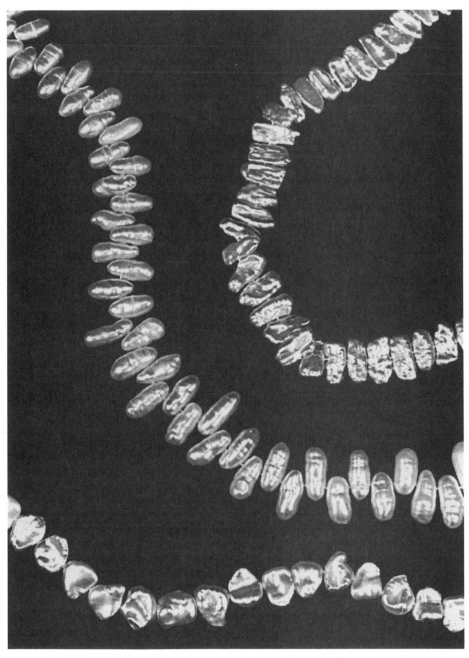

Fig. 11.5 Biwa pearls (Japanese cultured freshwater pearls)

It's not logical that a French wine should be more highly valued than one of equivalent quality from California. Neither is it logical that a gem or garment worn by a famous person should be worth more than one that isn't. Pricing, however, is not always logical. Perceptual and emotional factors also come into play.

When consumers ask about pearl pricing, they want to know how pearls are actually valued, not how they should be valued. In other words, they want to know the reality of the marketplace. Keeping this in mind, let's examine how the origin of freshwater pearls affects their value.

Biwa pearls versus those from other areas

When it comes to cultured freshwater pearls, those from Lake Biwa, Japan have the most prestige. This is because they tend to have a higher, more even luster and smoother surface than many of the pearls cultured in other areas. In addition, the mussels of Lake Biwa have produced larger quantities of high-quality pearls, and they have done so for a longer period of time.

Unfortunately, water pollution has brought the production of Biwa pearls to a halt. Now there are only a couple government experimental farms left. Some pearl dealers still sell Biwa pearls, which they bought before 1990. But for the most part, it's getting hard to find Biwa pearls, and they are starting to become collectors items. The finest strands of Biwa pearls can retail for over $15,000. As they become more scarce, their value could increase.

Chinese freshwater pearls are often the lowest priced due to low labor costs. Quality tends to be low, but China has produced a small percentage of high quality pearls. Some of these have been passed off as Biwa pearls. Due to better cultivating techniques, the quality of Chinese pearls has been rapidly improving. This has been particularly evident during the past couple of years. Examine Chinese freshwater pearls with an open mind. You may be pleasantly surprised to find attractive, high-quality pearls at reasonable prices. These prices, however, are rising.

Some distinctive natural and cultured freshwater pearls have been produced in the United States. Compared to Japan and China, however, pearl production has been low. For example, currently, it's hard to find American freshwater pearls in jewelry stores in Los Angeles--a major metropolitan area. Perhaps this will change as pearl production in the US increases.

Freshwater versus saltwater pearls

High-quality saltwater pearls tend to be more highly valued than those that are freshwater. There are some freshwater pearl producers that would disagree. Nevertheless, auction price records and the prices of pearls in jewelry stores indicate that saltwater pearls have commanded the highest prices.

Low prices, though, do not necessarily mean low quality. The $16 strand of Chinese rice pearls in figure 11.1 probably has a better luster, more orient, and a higher percentage of pearl nacre than the majority of cultured saltwater pearls on the market today. Therefore, don't just judge pearls by their price tag. Consider their luster, their color, their uniqueness. If you do, you'll discover that freshwater pearls offer great variety, beauty and value.

Chapter 11 Quiz

Select the correct answer.

1. Most cultured freshwater pearls come from:

a. Japan
b. Korea
c. China
d. USA

2. Most freshwater pearls are:

a. round
b. semi-round
c. oval
d. baroque

3. Which of the following freshwater pearl strands costs the least?

a. The top strand
b. The middle strand
c. The bottom strand

4. What factor affects the price of freshwater pearls the least?

a. luster
b. smoothness
c. size
d. body color

5. What determines the shape of a pearl?

a. The type of nucleus inserted in the mollusk.
b. The position of the nucleus in the mollusk.
c. The length of time the pearl is in the mollusk.
d. All of the above.

6. There is a wide difference of opinion as to what is the most valuable color for a freshwater pearl.

7. The price of freshwater pearls is often quoted according to their weight in grams.

8. A large flaw on a single freshwater pearl can lower its price significantly.

9. Iridescence and overtone colors are desirable characteristics for freshwater pearls.

10. High-quality freshwater pearls tend to cost more than high-quality saltwater pearls.

Answers:

1. c

2. d

3. c The bottom strand costs less due to its lack of smooth surfaces and smaller size. It also has a much lower luster, which is hard to determine from the photograph. The retail cost of this lower strand is about $2 as compared to $160 for the top strand.

4. d

5. d.

6. T

7. T

8. T

9. T

10. F   Freshwater pearls tend to cost less.

12

Imitation or Not?

Imagine a rosary-bead maker watching a fish being scaled in a basin of water. The water has colorful, pearly reflections which seem to form as the fish scales dissolve. The bead maker then gets the idea to filter the water, recover the pearly substance from it and mix it with a kind of varnish. Later he coats the inside surface of a hollow glass bead with the pearly mixture, fills the bead with wax, and what's the result? The birth of the modern-day imitation pearl.

This occurred in France in the 17th century. Jacquin was the name of the rosary-bead maker. And **essence of orient** (or **pearl essence**) is the name of the pearly mixture he discovered. Today, the finest imitation pearls usually have several coats of essence of orient.

Types of Imitation Pearls

Even though pearl essence is used to make many of the best imitation pearls, such as Majorica pearls. Imitations come in a variety of types. The main ones are:

♦ **Hollow glass beads containing wax.** These pearls, made by the same process as Jacquin's, are most likely to be found in antique jewelry.

♦ **Solid glass beads.** Majorica imitation pearls are an example of this type. They may be covered with as many as forty coats of pearl essence and hand polished between each coat. Imitation glass pearls are also coated with other substances such as synthetic pearl essence, plastic, cellulose, and lacquer.

♦ **Plastic beads.** These may have the same type coatings as the glass type. Plastic imitation pearl necklaces sometimes hang poorly due to their light weight.

♦ **Mother-of-pearl shell beads.** These are coated with the same substances as plastic and glass imitations. A coating made from powdered mother of pearl and synthetic resin may also be used. One company calls such beads **semi-cultured**. This is just a misleading term for imitation. Powdered mother-of-pearl coatings are not new. Centuries ago, American Indians produced imitation pearls by applying such coatings to clay beads and then baking them.

Occasionally, people sell uncoated mother-of-pearl beads as pearls or they describe them as very valuable. In the Pacific Islands, you can buy mother-of-pearl shell bead necklaces from the natives for a couple of dollars. Some of the better ones cost more.

Simulated and **faux pearls** (the French term for fake pearls) are two other terms used to designate imitation pearls. These pearls can be distinguished from natural and cultured pearls with the tests below.

Tests that Require No Equipment Other Than a Magnifier

Tooth Test Rub the pearls **lightly** along the biting edge of your upper front teeth. If they feel gritty or sandy, it's likely they are cultured or natural pearls. If they feel smooth, they are probably imitations.

There are a few problems with this test. It's not the most sanitary test. It may scratch the pearls, if done improperly. And it doesn't always work. There are some imitation pearls that feel gritty. Also, according to the Fall 1991 issue of *Gems & Gemology* (p. 176), real pearls may feel smooth. A cultured pearl sent to the GIA New York laboratory gave a smooth tooth test reaction because the surface had been polished. Therefore, don't rely solely on the tooth test. If you use it, combine it with the magnification tests listed below.

Surface Magnification Test Examine the surface of the pearl with a 10-power magnifier such as a loupe. If it looks grainy, like a photo take at an ISO of 1000 and above, there's a good chance it's an imitation (fig. 12.1). Pearls normally look unusually fine grained, like a photo taken at an ISO of 100 and below. Sometimes, though, dirt or pits on a pearl may make it seem to have a grainy appearance. Occasionally, too, freshwater and South Sea pearls may look a little grainy, but other surface characteristics mentioned in this section can prove they are not imitation.

If you have access to a microscope, also examine the surface at the highest possible magnification. At 50 power and above, a rough, pitted surface like the one in figure 12.2 means it's an imitation. Gas bubbles may also be present.

A surface with tiny, crooked lines giving it a scaly, maze-like appearance is characteristic of cultured and natural pearls (fig. 12.4). These scaly lines are not always evident at first. The surface may look smooth except for the flaws as in figure 12.3. Try using a strong, bare, direct light such as a fiber-optic; and shine it on the pearl from various angles to find the scaly lines. It's curious that pearls, which feel gritty to the teeth, can look so smooth under high magnification; whereas imitations, which feel smooth, tend to look coarse and rough. However, the less smooth an imitation is, the rougher it looks. On pearls, it's the "scaly-line" ridges that cause their gritty feel.

The best way to learn what the surface of pearls and imitations looks like under magnification is to examine many examples of each. When you can recognize how distinctive their surface textures are, you won't need to do any of the other tests to spot an imitation pearl.

Fig. 12.1 Note the grainy surface texture of this large imitation mabe pearl at 10-power magnification.

Fig. 12.2 Note how rough and pitted the surface of this imitation pearl looks at 64-power magnification

Fig. 12.3 Note how smooth the surface of this Akoya cultured pearl is at 64-power magnification compared to the imitation in fig. 12.2. Due to the lighting, scaly lines are not visible.

Fig. 12.4 Surface of a cultured black pearl at 64-power magnification. Note the scaly, terraced, maze-like patterns. They prove this is either a cultured or natural pearl. Due to the flattish baroque shape of this pearl, these patterns are visible with the fluorescent microscope light. On a round pearl like the one in figure 12.3, a strong, bare, pin-point light such as a fiberoptic may be necessary.

Drill Hole Test Examine the drill hole area with a magnifier of 10-power or above. (On some pearls, it may be hard to see into their drill hole.) Cultured pearls tend to show the following characteristics (figs. 12.5 - 12.8):

♦ There is often a clear dividing line between the pearl nacre and shell bead nucleus.
♦ The edges of the drill holes are often sharp and well defined. But when the nacre wears away it can leave the holes looking jagged and rough as in figures 12.7 and 12.8.
♦ The drill holes tend to be like a straight cylinder.
♦ The pearl nacre coating is normally thicker than the coating of imitations.

Imitation pearls tend to show these characteristics (figs 12.9 - 12.12):

♦ There is normally no dark dividing line between the coating and the rest of the pearl. Occasionally, one may see a kind of line, but the other characteristics of the drill hole will look like those of imitations. If you are in doubt, look at the drill hole opening on the other side of the pearl and on other pearls of the strand.

♦ The coating around the edges of the drill holes may have flaked off, making it look ragged or uneven.

♦ The drill holes may be angled outward at the surface of the pearl. Other times the drill holes may round inward at the surface and bow outward inside the pearl.

♦ The coating often looks like a thin coat of shiny paint. The thinness can be seen at the edge of the drill hole or around bare areas which expose the inner bead.

♦ Rounded ridges may have formed around the drill hole (figs. 12.11 & 12.12).

♦ If the bead is made of glass, its glassy luster may be apparent.

Flaw Test

Examine the pearls for flaws. If they appear flawless, this is a sign they are imitation. Also note the types of flaws present. Many of those found on cultured pearls look different from those on imitations. If you examine pearl flaws with a 10-power magnifier whenever possible, it will be easier for you to recognize them. Chapter 6 shows examples of pearl flaws.

Overtone Test

Look for overtone colors in the pearls. Imitations frequently have none, and when they do, the overtones all tend to look the same. It's normal for cultured and natural pearls to have overtones, and these overtones often vary in color within the strand (color photo #2).

Besides examining the overtones with the naked eye, also look at them with a loupe. The magnification makes the coloring differences between imitations and real pearls even more apparent.

Matching Test

Note the shape, luster, size, and color of the pearls. Imitations often seem perfectly matched, whereas there tend to be variations among the pearls on cultured or natural strands.

Heaviness Test

Bounce the pearls in your hand. If they feel unusually light, they're most likely made of plastic or filled with wax. Solid glass beads may feel heavier or about the same as cultured and natural pearls.

Clasp Test

Is the clasp made of silver, steel, or a gold plated metal. This is a warning sign that the strand may be imitation. But good pearls are occasionally strung with cheap clasps and imitation ones with expensive clasps.

Price Test

Is the price of the pearls unbelievably low? If so, they may be imitation or have hardly any pearl nacre. Jewelers can't stay in business if they sell their pearls below their cost.

Fig. 12.5 Note the sharp, well-defined edges of the drill hole. The line between the nacre and nucleus is hard to see due to the thickness of the nacre and the small size of the hole.

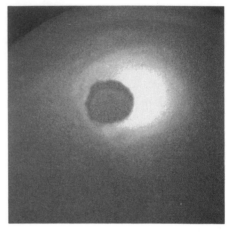

Fig. 12.6 A straight drill hole and the separation line between the core and thin nacre indicate this is a cultured pearl.

Fig. 12.7 The coating of both cultured and imitation pearls can wear away at the drill hole and look ragged. But pearl nacre has a distinctive appearance and is usually thicker than that of imitations.

Fig. 12.8 The nacre has separated from the core in this pearl. A separation like this would not be characteristic of an imitation pearl.

Drill Holes of Imitation Pearls

Fig. 12.9 The very thin ragged coating, angled-in drill hole, and lack of dividing line between core and coating indicate this is an imitation.

Fig. 12.10 The distinctive appearance of the coating, lack of dividing line, and the drill-hole which bows outward inside (not visible in photo) mean this is an imitation.

Fig. 12.11 Swirly formations around the drill hole, very thin glossy coating, and lack of dividing line are clues this coated mother-of-pearl shell bead is an imitation.

Fig. 12.12 Another imitation with a mother-of-pearl shell bead nucleus.

Other Tests

X-radiograph Test

An x-ray photo called an **x-radiograph** is taken of the pearls. Imitations are opaque to x-rays making them look solid white on the negative and solid black on the positive print made of it. Cultured and natural pearls are semitransparent to x-rays and usually look grayish.

Since imitations pearls can be positively identified with other tests, x-raying them is usually a waste of money. There is, however, a major advantage to the x-ray test. It's quicker to x-ray an entire strand at once than to test each pearl in it individually.

Refractometer Test

The "pearl" is placed on a refractometer (an instrument that measures a gem's **refractive index**--the degree to which light is bent as it passes through the gem). A pearl will generally have a low reading of 1.530 and a high one of 1.685. The numerical difference between these two readings is .155 and is called its **birefringence**. Pearls have an unusually high birefringence compared to other gems. This causes a blinking and pink effect when their refractive index is read through a rotating Polaroid filter. The GIA Pearls Course states that the presence of this "birefringent blink" is proof a pearl is not an imitation.

The refractive index of some imitations can also prove they are not cultured or natural pearls. For example, the Majorica imitation pearls the GIA tested for their Fall 1990 article in *Gems and Gemology* had a refractive index of 1.48, which was a conclusive means of identification.

Distinguishing between imitations and pearls is not hard. Even laypeople can learn how to detect imitations with a loupe, but they do need practice. What's hard is to distinguish cultured pearls from those that are natural. This will be the focus of the next chapter.

Chapter 12 Quiz

Select the correct answer.

1. A strand feels light in weight. There's a good chance it consists of:

a. Cultured pearls with thin nacre
b. Natural pearls
c. Plastic imitation pearls
d. Solid glass imitation pearls

2. Which of the following tests can prove that your pearls are not imitations?

a. The tooth test.
b. The surface magnification test
c. The overtone test
d. All of the above

3. Which is a typical characteristic of the drill holes of imitation pearls.

a. a clear dividing line between the coating and the core of the "pearl."
b. a straight hole with well defined edges
c. a thick coating of lacquer, paint, or pearl essence.
d. none of the above

4. Which of the following is an imitation pearl?

a. A semi-cultured pearl
b. A Majorica pearl
c. A faux pearl
d. b and c
e. a, b, and c

5. Under 10-power magnification the surface of an imitation pearl tends to:

a. look grainy
b. show scaly maze-like patterns
c. appear striped
d. none of the above

6. If a jeweler can't tell that the pearls you are wearing are imitation or not this means:

a. He's a lousy jeweler.
b. He needs to read *The Pearl Buying Guide.*
c. He must have poor eyesight.
d. All of the above
e. None of the above.

7. Which of the two strands below is most likely imitation. Explain your answer.

a. top strand
b. bottom strand

Answers:

1. c

2. b   The results of the tooth and overtone tests are good indications but they don't provide positive proof. Some imitations feel gritty to the teeth and have overtones that vary. Thin-nacre pearls may have no overtones, and polished pearls may give a smooth tooth-test reaction.

3. d   The coating on imitation pearls tends to be very thin, not thick.

4. e   Majorica, faux, and semi-cultured pearls are all imitations.

5. a

6. e   Even pearl specialists can be fooled by imitations, particularly when viewing pearls from a distance. In some cases, they may need to examine the pearls under magnification to determine that they are imitation.

7. a   The top strand is in fact imitation. It would be hard to find natural or cultured pearls that are so round and perfectly matched (some pearl strands, however, are exceptionally well-matched).

     Note the slight irregularities of shape, size, luster, and depth of color in the bottom strand. This is typical of cultured pearls. A natural pearl strand would tend to be even more irregular. Variations among pearls on a strand do not prove they are real. Sometimes imitations are poorly matched.

13

Natural or Cultured?

In 1917, Cartier bought their building in New York with two strands of natural pearls valued at a million dollars. In 1957, the pearls were sold at auction for $157,000. Perhaps one of the main reasons for this drop in price, was the introduction of the cultured pearl, which decreased the demand for natural pearls.

Prices of natural pearls have risen considerably since 1957, but they still don't match those of the early 1900's. Nevertheless, natural pearls are still worth a lot more than cultured pearls. Therefore, it's important to be able to distinguish between them. X-ray tests are generally required to prove a pearl is natural, but they are costly. Other tests can help you determine a pearl is cultured and thereby save you the expense of an x-ray. These tests are listed below. Keep in mind that almost all the pearls produced today are cultured. You are most likely to find natural pearls in antique pieces. (Whole pearls were not cultured before the 1900's.) However, the natural pearls in antique jewelry may have been replaced with cultured ones.

Tests a Layperson Can Do

Drill Hole Test   Look inside the drill hole with a 10-power magnifier. If you can see a dark dividing line separating the nacre from a pearl bead nucleus, the pearl is cultured. Natural pearls may show a series of growth lines, which get more yellow or brown towards the center of the pearl. A black deposit at the center of a white pearl can be a sure sign the pearl is natural. (From *Gem Testing* by B W Anderson, page 219.)

Also note the size of the drill hole. The drill holes of natural pearls are rarely larger than .04 mm (.016 inch). Those of cultured pearls tend to measure .06 mm (.024 inch). (From *Pearls* by Jean Taburiaux, page 193.)

Shape Test

Do the pearls look perfectly round? If so, then it's likely they are cultured. Natural pearls tend to have at least slightly irregular shapes, even though a few are round. This test is only an indication. It is not proof.

Blink Test

Hold the strand near the front edge of a strong desk lamp. The light should shine through the pearls but not in your eyes. Rotate the strand. If the pearls blink from light to dark as they are turned, this indicates they are cultured and have a thin coating of nacre (imitation pearls with mother-of-pearl shell-bead centers may also blink). The dark areas result when mother of pearl layers on the shell bead block the light. Figure 13.1 shows light and dark views of shell beads with transmitted light. Thin-nacre cultured pearls may show only one view when rotated. In other words, they don't necessarily blink.

Fig. 13.1 Dark and light views of mother-of-pearl shell beads

Fig. 13.2 Stripes in a thin-nacre cultured pearl viewed with transmitted light

Stripe Test

As you rotate the pearls with strong light shining through them, look for curved lines and stripes (fig. 13.2). These are the layers of the shell beads. If they are visible, the nacre is very thin and the pearls are cultured. Not all shell bead nuclei show stripes, though. This can be seen in figure 13.3. Keep in mind that imitation pearls with shell-bead centers can also display this banded effect. Natural pearls, however, will not look striped.

Color Test

Examine the color. Cultured pearls often have a faint greenish tint, unlike natural pearls. Some people say the color of cultured pearls tends to be less even than that of natural pearls. Color can only suggest a pearl might be cultured. It is not proof.

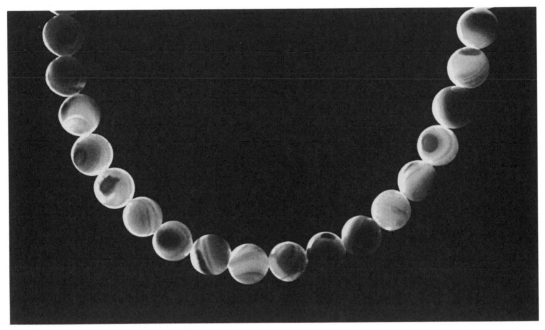

Fig. 13.3 Mother-of-pearl shell beads (the core of cultured pearls) seen with transmitted light

Other Tests

X-radiograph Test This is the most reliable way to distinguish between natural and cultured pearls. On an x-radiograph negative, cultured pearls usually show a clear separation between core and nacre. Plus, their core normally looks lighter than the nacre coating. X-rayed natural pearls tend to either look the same tone throughout or get darker in their center. A mantle tissue nucleus will look like a very dark, irregular-shaped void.

The disadvantage of x-ray tests is that it can cost between $100 and $300 to have them done, and there are few gem labs that have the required equipment.

X-ray Fluorescence Test This test is used in combination with an x-radiograph to provide the added information of whether the pearl is freshwater or saltwater. Natural saltwater pearls rarely fluoresce to x-rays, whereas natural freshwater pearls have a fairly strong x-ray fluorescence, usually moderate to strong yellowish white. (Cultured saltwater pearls with a freshwater shell-bead nucleus fluoresce moderately strong to very weak, depending on nacre thickness.)

Non-nucleus cultured Biwa pearls have a distinct fluorescent color and a longer phosphorescence (after glow) than cultured salt-water pearls, which show a greenish yellow fluorescence. Cultured pearls dyed with silver salts show usually show no fluorescence.

Specific Gravity Test The pearls are placed in a liquid that has a specific gravity of 2.71 (purchased at gem instrument stores and tested with a piece of pure calcite). The majority of natural pearls will float and others will sink slowly. Most cultured pearls with shell nuclei will sink quickly since they tend to be heavier than natural pearls. The biggest problem with this test is that the heavy liquid may damage the pearls, especially if the pearls are left in it too long.

UV Fluorescence Test The pearls are placed under long-wave ultraviolet light and compared to known samples of cultured and natural pearls. In his book *Gemstones* (p. 448), G F Herbert Smith mentions how cultured pearls can display a peculiar greenish fluorescence which differs markedly from the sky-blue effect of many natural pearls. He points out that this is not an infallible test because natural pearls can also have a greenish fluorescence, particularly if they are from waters adjacent to those of cultured pearls. Consequently, gem labs with x-ray equipment do not use this test. However, this test may help those without x-ray machines. Seeing a unique sky-blue fluorescence under LW UV light instead of a greenish-yellow glow may serve as an additional incentive to pay for an x-ray to test for natural origin. (This test is also mentioned in Webster's *Gems* on page 539.)

If the pearls are of good quality and preliminary tests suggest they may be natural, then it's advisable to have them x-rayed. Appraisers and jewelers can send them to the appropriate labs for you. Some of the gem labs that have the facilities to do x-ray tests are listed below. Jewelers in your area may know of others.

Gem Testing Laboratory of Great Britain
27 Greville Street (Saffron Hill Entrance)
London EC1N8SU   Tel. (071) 405-3351

GIA Gem Trade Laboratory, Inc.
1630 Stewart Street
Santa Monica, CA 90404 Tel. (310) 828-3148
        or
580 Fifth Ave.
New York, NY 10036   Tel. (212) 221-5858

Gubelin Gemmological Laboratory
Maihofstrasse 102
CH-6000 Lucerne 9   Switzerland Tel. 041/26 17 17

The Laboratory
2 Place de la Bourse
75002 Paris

Swiss Gemmological Institute
Lowenstrasse 17
CH-8001 Zurich   Tel. 01-211-24-71

Chapter 13 Quiz

Select the correct answer:

1. As you rotate a strand of "pearls" under a light, they blink and/or show faint stripes. This indicates the "pearls" are:

a. imitation
b. cultured
c. natural
d. imitation or cultured

2. You are examining a "pearl." Its drill hole looks ragged and some of the coating has peeled off around it. This means the "pearl" is:

a. imitation.
b. cultured.
c. either imitation or cultured.
d. either cultured or natural.

3. Which of the following can help a gemologist distinguish between natural and cultured pearls?

a. An X-ray test
b. A refractometer test
c. A hardness test
d. All of the above

4. Natural pearls:

a. tend to be very round
b. tend to have greenish overtones
c. tend to have smaller drill holes than cultured pearls and imitations.
d. None of the above.

5. An appraiser tells you your pearls must be sent to another lab for an x-ray in order to determine if they are natural. The appraiser:

a. is not very competent.
b. has a poorly equipped lab.
c. is trying to make extra money on unnecessary lab tests.
d. is correct, and this does not mean that he/she is a poor appraiser.

True or False?

6. If an antique pearl piece was made before 1900, the pearls in it are natural.

7. Most cultured pearls tend to be slightly heavier than natural pearls.

8. Natural pearls tend to have irregular shapes.

9. If a pearl does not blink or show stripes when it is rotated under an overhead light, then it is not cultured.

10. The nacre of cultured pearls has a different chemical composition than that of natural pearls.

Answers:

1. d   Imitation pearls with shell cores and translucent coatings can show stripes like those of thin-nacre cultured pearls.

2. c.   The coating can peel off of both imitation and cultured pearls leaving their core exposed.

3. a

4. c

5. d

6. F   When natural pearls fall out of antique pieces, they are often replaced with cultured pearls or imitations.

7. T

8. T

9. F   Cultured pearls with thick nacre or with no shell nucleus normally don't blink or show stripes. Not all cultured pearls with thin nacre display the blinking or striped effect.

10. F

14

Choosing the Clasp

Mrs. Kirk was proud of the beautiful pearl necklace her daughter had given her, but she hardly ever wore it. She had arthritis, and that made it hard for her to fasten and undo the clasp. Since she lived by herself, nobody was around to help her put on the necklace, so it was easier to leave it in her jewelry box.

Mrs. Kirk is not alone. Complicated or hard-to-fasten clasps keep a lot of people from wearing some of their jewelry pieces. This could be prevented with a bit of forethought. When choosing a clasp, consider:

- How secure is it?
- How easy is it to open?
- How versatile is it?
- How much does it cost?

Determine what is most important to you about the clasp because normally, some compromises will have to be made. For example, to get a clasp that is easy to open, you may have to accept less security.

Fig. 14.1 Fish-hook clasp

Fig. 14.2 Push clasp

Fig. 14.3 Screw clasp (mystery clasp)

Fig. 14.4 Pin pearl adaptor

Listed below are three basic pearl clasps along with their advantages and disadvantages.

♦ **Fish-hook clasp** (fig 14.1): This is a popular clasp because it's inexpensive and secure. It may be silver, gold, or gold-plated. The main drawback of the fish-hook clasp is that it can be hard to undo, especially for someone with arthritis.

♦ **Push clasp** (fig. 14.2): The main advantage of this clasp, is that it is fairly easy to open, even with one hand when it's used on a bracelet. It's also relatively inexpensive. Unfortunately, it is not as secure as some of the other clasps.

♦ **The screw clasp** (fig. 14.3): This clasp can add versatility when it is inserted in pearls to form a **hidden or mystery clasp**. For example, a long strand of pearls with three mystery clasps can be unscrewed and turned into a bracelet and two smaller necklaces.

    Mystery clasps are fairly easy to open and close and are secure, provided they are screwed in all the way and are not stripped out. They tend to cost a little more than the fish-hook and push clasps.

    Sometimes the string breaks on necklaces with mystery clasps. This can happen when people unscrew the clasp incorrectly or when they can't find the clasp and try to unscrew the necklace in a spot where there is no clasp. This problem can be avoided by having the jeweler show you how to find and open the clasp. When undoing it, be sure to grasp at least two pearls on either side of the clasp. Turn them together as a unit. Don't twist the string.

    There are a wide variety of clasps besides these three basic ones. Some are both decorative and versatile (figs. 14.5 & 14.6).

Fig. 14.5 A hinged clasp, trademarked **Applaudere** by A & Z Pearls Inc. Note how each end of the strand is attached to a clasp. The pair of clasps can be fastened over any of the pearls on the necklace allowing a variety of styles from a single strand of pearls. See Chapter 15 for examples.

Fig. 14.6 A clasp that can be worn to the side, front or back with one to three strands. It forms part of a pearl linking system which allows a rope-length strand to also be worn as a three strand choker or an opera length necklace. This system is trade-marked **Multipearls** by Mastoloni Cultured Pearls. Photo courtesy Frank Mastoloni & Sons, Inc.

Many clasps are jewelry pieces by themselves and are best worn to the side or in the front. Figure 14.5 is an example of this.

Sometimes accessories are used to accent pearls with plain clasps. With the **pin pearl adaptor** (see figure 4.4), a pin can be attached to two strands to look like a decorative clasp or it can be worn as a pearl shortener (see fig. 15.7 in the next chapter). The pin pearl adaptor slides on to any pin and then can be closed over two strands of pearls.

One of the most popular pearl accessories is the **pearl enhancer**. It is a pendant which can be attached to a strand of pearls, as well to as a gold chain or bead necklace. The top of the pearl enhancer has a hinged clasp which closes over the necklace between two pearls (see fig. 15.14 in the next chapter).

Fig. 14.7 Pearl enhancer

Fig. 14.8 Freshwater pearl necklace clasped with an antique mother-of-pearl gambling chip. The piece portrays a scene from Chinese life and was probably carved during the 19th century.

There are many other types and styles of clasps besides the ones pictured in this chapter. You can see them on display in jewelry stores. No matter what type you choose do not take a necklace or bracelet home without first having the salesperson show you how to fasten and unfasten the clasp. Then try doing it at least two times by yourself. Some clasps are like puzzles, and if you try to figure them out on your own, you could damage the clasp and/or the pearls.

If your budget is limited, put your money into the pearls first, rather than into a fancy clasp. You can always upgrade the clasp later on. When buying a pearl necklace, your first priority should be the pearls.

15

Versatile Ways to Wear a Strand of Pearls

There are no other gems that offer more versatility than pearls. Queen Elizabeth I of England made the most of this feature. She wore yards of them as necklaces hanging down as far her knees. She had them threaded in her wigs, embroidered in her clothing, and set in her crown and other regal jewelry. You can also enjoy the versatility of pearls. The styles listed below and shown in figures 15.1 - 15.15 can be made with just one opera-length necklace (about 28 to 34 inches) and a pair of hinged clasps like the Applaudere, pictured in figure 14.5 of the previous chapter.

♦ A single strand of adjustable lengths with the clasp in the back (fig. 15.1)
♦ A double strand on one side and single on the other (fig. 15.2)
♦ A double strand choker or princess necklace (fig. 15.3)
♦ A single strand clasped to form one "chain" hanging in the front. (fig. 15.4). An opera-length strand can be worn as a belt in the same manner.
♦ A single strand tied or knotted in front to form two "chains" hanging in the front (fig. 15.5)
♦ Double strand in back and triple strand in the front (fig. 15.6)
♦ A single strand looped in the front with a pearl shortener (fig. 15.7)
♦ Double strand in front and single strand in back (fig. 15.8)
♦ Double strand looped together in front (fig. 15.9)
♦ Single strand with a clasp to the side or in the center (fig. 15.10)
♦ Single strand knotted in the front (fig. 15.11). Dresses with low V-backs can be accented with a rope-length strand tied like this in the back.

Fig. 15.1

Fig. 15.2

Fig. 15.3

Fig. 15.4

Fig. 15.5

Fig. 15.6

Fig. 15.7

Fig. 15.8

Fig. 15.9

Fig. 15.10

Fig. 15.11

Fig. 15.12

Fig. 15.13

Fig. 15.14

Fig. 15.15

Fig. 15.16 Photo courtesy of the Cultured Pearl
Associations of America & Japan

Fig. 15.17 Photo courtesy Cultured Pearl
Associations of America & Japan

Fig. 15.18 Photo courtesy Cultured Pearl
Associations of America & Japan

- Double strand twisted and clasped in the back (fig. 15.12)
- Double strand with a loop hanging in the front like a pendant (fig. 15.13)
- Double or single strand with a pearl enhancer (detachable pendant) (fig. 15.14)
- Multi-strand bracelet (fig. 15.15)
- Wrapped in the hair around a chignon or ponytail (fig. 15.16)
- Attached to the side with a pin and hanging asymmetrically
- Pinned across a V-back dress or sweater

Other options are possible with longer or multi-piece necklaces. For example:

- Attached to the shoulders of a dress as in figure 15.17
- Looped through button-holes or openings in clothing as in figure 15.18
- Wrapped around a hat

These are only some of the ways pearls can be worn. Use your imagination and you'll discover many more.

16

Caring for Your Pearls

Which of the following is hardest and which is softest?

♦ A pearl
♦ An opal
♦ Pure gold
♦ A tooth

The hardest is the opal. It has a hardness of 5 1/2 - 6 1/2 on the Moh's scale, which rates the relative hardness of materials from 1 to 10. (The 10 rating of a diamond is the highest, but a diamond is over 1000 times harder than an opal.) **Hardness** is a material's resistance to scratching and abrasions.

The softest of the four materials above is pure gold, which has a hardness of 2 - 2 1/2. When alloyed with other metals, the hardness of gold increases, but it is still a relatively soft metal.

Tooth enamel has a hardness of 5, and a pearl has a range of 2 1/2 - 4. In other words, a pearl is a relatively soft material.

Knowing how soft a pearl is can help us understand why pearls should not be tossed on top of or next to other gems in a jewelry box. Knowing that a tooth is harder than a pearl helps us understand why the "tooth test" for identifying imitations should only be done very lightly or else avoided. The basic concept of hardness is that a harder material will scratch one that is softer.

Besides being soft, pearls are easily damaged by chemicals or eaten away by acids such as vinegar and lemon juice. Heat can turn pearls brown or dry them out and make them crack.

One advantage of pearls is they are fairly tough considering their softness. In his book *Pearls*, Alexander Farn relates how jewelers and pearl merchants of old would separate imitation pearls from real ones by having footmen stomp on them. Those that were crushed were imitation. The natural pearls normally would resist such blows. Cultured pearls, especially those with thin nacre, are not this durable. Therefore, it's best to avoid dropping or crushing them.

Cleaning Your Pearls

The softness of pearls and their low resistance to heat and chemicals mean that special precautions must be taken when cleaning them. Keep in mind the following guidelines:

♦ Do not use commercial jewelry cleaners on pearls unless the labels say they are safe for pearls. Many of them contain ammonia, which will cause deterioration.

♦ Never clean pearls in an ultrasonic cleaner. It can damage the pearls and wash out the color if the pearls have been dyed.

♦ Never steam-clean pearls. Heat can harm them.

♦ Never use detergents, bleaches, powdered cleansers, baking soda, or ammonia-based cleaners on pearls.

♦ Do not use toothbrushes, scouring pads, or abrasive materials to clean pearls. They can scratch their surface. If there's a lump of dirt that can't be rubbed off with a soft cloth, try using your fingernails. They have a hardness of only 2 1/2 or less.

Cleaning pearls is not complicated. After you wear them just wipe them off with a soft cloth or chamois which can be dry or damp. This will prevent the dirt from accumulating and keep perspiration, which is slightly acidic, from eating away at the pearl nacre.

If the pearls have not been kept clean and are very dirty, they can be cleaned by your jeweler or they can be washed in water and a mild soap such as Ivory or Lux liquid (some liquid soaps, such as Dawn, can damage pearls) and cleaned with a soft cloth. Pay attention to the areas around the drill holes where dirt may tend to collect. After washing them, lay the pearls flat in a moist kitchen towel to dry. After the towel is dry, they should be dry. Do not wear pearls when their string is wet. Wet strings stretch and attract dirt which is hard to remove. Likewise do not hang pearls to dry.

Storing Your Pearls

Pearls are composed of about 2 to 4% water along with calcium carbonate and an organic binder called conchiolin. If the pearls become dehydrated, they can get brittle and crack. Consequently, they should not be kept near heaters or in places that get strong sunlight, such as on a window sill. Safe deposit boxes can be unusually dry, so if you ever store pearls there, try to take them out occasionally and expose them to humidity or moisture. Sealed plastic bags are not the best place for pearls. They can keep them from breathing and getting moisture.

Since pearls are soft, they should be kept in something that will protect them from scratches. Jewelry pouches or cloth bags are ideal. Pearls can also be wrapped in soft material and kept wherever convenient. Jewelry boxes may be handy, but they are also the first place burglars look.

Having Your Pearls Strung

Pearl necklaces can stretch with time and the string can get dirty and weak. Thus, they should be restrung periodically--about once a year, but that depends on how often they are worn. Fine pearls should be strung with silk and with knots tied between each pearl. This prevents them from rubbing against each other and from scattering if the string should break.

Occasionally pearls are strung with gold beads. According to a Los Angeles pearl stringer, gold turns pearls ivory-colored and coral black, and this is a permanent discoloration. Therefore, it's not advisable to string expensive pearls with gold beads.

Miscellaneous Tips

♦ Take your pearls off when applying cosmetics, hair sprays, and perfume. These beauty aids are made of chemicals and acids which can harm your pearls.

♦ Take your pearls off when showering or swimming. It's not good to get the string wet, plus the chlorine or soap can damage the pearls. Pearl rings should be taken off when washing your hands or the dishes. Put the ring in a protective container or safe spot where it won't accidentally fall in the drain or get lost.

♦ When selecting pearl jewelry, check to see if the pearl is mounted securely. Preferably, the pearl will have been drilled and glued to a post on the mounting, especially if it is a ring. Otherwise, the pearl may come loose. If the pearl is flawless, a drill hole could lower it's value. In such a case, it would be safer to set the undrilled pearl in a pin, pendant or earring than in a ring.

- When taking off a pearl ring, grasp the shank or metal part rather than the pearl. This will prevent the pearl from loosening and coming into contact with skin oil on your hand.

- Avoid wearing pearls with rough fabrics such as Shetland wool. They can scratch the pearls.

- About every six months, have a jewelry professional verify that the pearls on your jewelry are securely mounted or that the string is still good. Many jewelers will do this free of charge, and they'll be happy to answer your questions regarding the care of your jewelry.

Chapter 16 Quiz

True or False?

1. The best way to clean pearls is to put them in an ultrasonic cleaner.

2. You should take your pearls off when you shower or go swimming.

3. Decorative gold beads strung between pearls never damage or discolor the pearls.

4. The pearl is an ideal gem for an every-day wedding ring.

5. You should put on make-up and perfume before you put on your pearls.

6. Pearls should **not** be worn when their string is wet.

7. It doesn't matter if hair spray gets on your pearls because the lacquer makes them more lustrous and serves as a protective coating.

8. After wearing pearls, it's a good idea to wipe them off with a chamois.

Answers:

1. F   Pearls should never be placed in ultrasonic cleaners.

2. T

3. F

4. F

5. T

6. T

7. F

8. T

17

Finding a Good Buy

Charlene is in a jewelry store. She's telling Scott, the owner, that she wants a nice pearl necklace but she's on a very limited budget. Although she's looked elsewhere, she hasn't found a strand she likes at a good price.

Scott first shows her a strand of Japanese saltwater pearls. He points out that the pearls are round and well matched, but their pearl coating is very thin. Consequently the strand is not a good choice for long-term, every-day wear. He adds that the round white saltwater pearls in her price range tend to have a thin coating, no matter where they're sold. Charlene wonders why no other jewelers ever mentioned this to her.

Scott then shows her some strands of freshwater pearls and asks her to compare them to the first strand. They're a lot more lustrous. Then he helps Charlene pick out an affordable strand that looks good on her. Charlene is impressed with Scott's selection of pearls and his straightforward approach. She plans on coming back to him for the rest of her jewelry needs, including a strand of good saltwater pearls when she has more to spend.

Jeff wants to buy his wife some pearls for their 30th anniversary, since this is the traditional gift. He and his wife have been happily married for many years, so he wants the pearls to be of unusually fine quality. Jeff has read *The Pearl Buying Guide* and is aware that pearls have many subtle quality differences. He realizes he will need some expert help.

As he shops, he discovers that he knows more than a lot of the salespeople. Eventually, Jeff finds somebody who is really knowledgeable about pearls--Sandy, a college student who works part-time to pay her way through school. Sandy has always had a keen interest in gems, especially pearls, and she takes advantage of every opportunity to learn as much as possible about them.

Jeff already knows that he wants either pink or white saltwater pearls in the 7 to 8 millimeter range. Sandy brings out a variety of strands and points out the fine nuances of luster, color, and surface markings. Then she helps him choose two strands, which they will have strung with three mystery clasps. That way his wife can wear the pearls in different necklace lengths and as a bracelet. This is a quick and easy sale for Sandy, and it's a pleasant experience for Jeff. He's gotten efficient, professional help and exactly the kind of pearls he was looking for.

Erica is in a Tahitian jewelry store looking through a bowl of black pearls. Before coming to Tahiti on holiday, she read *The Pearl Buying Guide*. The salesman in the store tells her that she can have any of the pearls in the bowl for the equivalent of $120. Erica first picks out the ones with the best luster. Then she eliminates those that are either too light or have no overtone colors. Finally, she ends up with a fairly large, tear-drop-shaped, dark-gray pearl with some greenish and purplish highlights. One side of the pearl, however, is badly flawed. But Erica plans to wear it as a pendant, so the flaws won't show.

On the flight back home, she sketches a design for the pendant and then later has her jeweler make it. He tells her he could never find a black pearl as attractive as hers for such a low price. When the pendant is finished, Erica tries it on. She's very pleased with how it looks. But she's even more pleased that she owns a unique piece which she has helped create.

Shopping for pearls turned out to be a positive experience for Erica, Jeff, and Charlene. This was largely because they took the time to learn about pearls beforehand and/or they dealt with a competent salesperson. Listed below are some guidelines that helped them and can help you when you shop for pearls.

♦ **Look for luster.** This was the first quality factor that Erica focused her attention on because it's the most important one. To understand why, just compare dull milky pearls to some highly lustrous ones. Chapter 4 gives you tips on judging luster.

♦ **When judging prices, try to compare pearls of the same type, shape, size, color, luster, and blemish quality.** All of these factors affect the cost of pearls. Due to the complexity of pearl pricing, it's easier for consumers to compare pearls that are alike or at least similar.

♦ **Look at a variety of qualities** so you'll have a basis for comparison.

♦ **Remember that there is no standardized system for grading pearls.** As a consequence, grades such as "A" have no meaning other than what the seller assigns to them. In some cases, an "A" grade may be the lowest quality a store stocks. The lack of standardization does not mean there's no point in grading pearls. It's just an added reason why you need to know how to judge pearl quality yourself.

♦ **Be willing to compromise.** Both Charlene and Erica had to settle for something other than what they might have preferred in order to stay within their budget. Charlene got freshwater instead of saltwater pearls. Erica's pearl was badly flawed on one side. Even people with unlimited budgets have to compromise sometimes on the size, shape, color, or quality due to lack of availability. A pearl doesn't have to be perfect for you to enjoy it.

♦ **Beware of sales ads that seem too good to be true.** The advertised pearls might be of unacceptable quality, especially in terms of nacre thickness. Or they might be stolen or misrepresented. Jewelers are in business to make money, not to lose it.

♦ **If possible, establish a relationship with a jeweler** you can trust and who looks after your interests. He can help you find buys you wouldn't find on your own.

♦ **Place the pearls against your hand and answer the following questions.** A negative answer suggests the pearls are a poor choice.

a. Do the pearls have bright, sharp light reflections?
b. Do the pearls have overtone colors? (This is a characteristic of pearls with good luster.)
c. Does the color of the pearls look good next to your skin?

The above guidelines in essence suggest that you learn how to evaluate pearls. But why is it so important for you to do this? Why should jewelers educate you about pearl quality? Is it just to help you compare prices?

No. Learning more about pearls will help you make a choice you can enjoy for a lifetime and will help you appreciate the unique qualities of the pearls you choose. How can you appreciate something you don't understand?

As you learn to compare luster differences among pearls, you will see how pearl brilliance differs from that of other gems. The brilliance of faceted gems normally appears best in their face-up position. No matter how you hold or wear good pearls, they glow. Even away from light they glow. And this glow has an intensity and depth unmatched by any other shiny round object.

As you learn to compare the color nuances of pearls, you'll see that good pearls are not just white. They have a variety of underlying colors which add to their beauty. And they come in a wide spectrum of body colors. Some people say that pearls make them look washed out. These people change their mind when they see black pearls and when they try on lighter pearls that enhance their body coloring.

As you are introduced to the different pearl shapes, you'll see how pearls offer creative design possibilities unlike any other gem. Even a basic strand of round pearls can be worn in creative, versatile ways.

Pearls can be worn anywhere, at any time, with anything. And even though pearls offer all these positive features, you don't have to be rich to own fine-quality pearls. If you are willing to compromise on the type of pearls you choose, you should be able to find good ones to fit almost any budget.

But to spot good pearls, you need to know how to judge their quality. So look at pearls whenever possible. Take time to analyze them. Ask jewelers to explain their quality differences. Gradually, you'll learn to recognize good value, and you'll see that the pearl is a remarkable gem which has no peer.

Appendix

Chemical, Physical, & Optical Characteristics of Pearls

(The information below is mainly based on the following three sources:

Gems by Robert Webster
GIA Gem Reference Guide
GIA Colored Stones Course, Chapters 13 & 14 (1980 version)

Chemical composition:	$CaCO_3$ (most of it aragonite, the rest calcite) 82 to 92 % H_2O 2 to 4% Conchiolin 4 to 14% Other about 0.4%
Mohs' hardness:	2 1/2 to 4
Specific gravity:	White natural saltwater pearls: 2.66 - 2.76 except for some Australian pearls whose density may be as high as 2.78 Black natural saltwater pearls (Gulf of California): 2.61 - 2.69 Natural freshwater pearls: 2.66 - 2.78 Japanese Akoya cultured pearls: 2.72 - 2.78 or more Mantle-tissue nucleated cultured pearls: 2.67 - 2.70
Toughness:	Usually good, but variable. Old, dehydrated, or excessively bleached pearls are not as tough.
Cleavage:	None
Fracture:	Uneven
Streak:	White

Crystal character:	An aggregate composed mostly of tiny orthorhombic (pseudo-hexagonal) aragonite crystals and sometimes hexagonal calcite crystals. Conchiolin, an organic binding material, is noncrystalline.
Optic Character:	AGG, if not opaque (also listed as doubly refractive)
Refractive Index:	1.530 - 1.685
Birefringence:	.155
Dispersion:	None
Luster:	Dull to almost metallic. Fractures may look pearly to dull.
Phenomena:	Orient. Varies from almost none to very noticeable.
Pleochroism:	None
Chelsea-filter reaction:	None
Absorption spectra:	Varies greatly, not diagnostic
Ultraviolet fluorescence:	None to strong light blue, yellow, green, or pink under both LW and SW. Natural color black pearls - weak to moderate red to orangy red under LW.
Reaction to heat:	Pearls can burn, split, crack, or turn brown in excessive heat such as an open flame. Prolonged heat may cause dehydration, which may cause the nacre to crack.
Reaction to chemicals:	Attacked by all acids. Lotions, cosmetics, perspiration, and perfumes can also damage the nacre.
Stability to light:	Stable except for some dyed pearls.
Effect of irradiation:	Darkens color
Transparency to x-rays:	Semitransparent
X-ray fluorescence:	Natural saltwater pearls--inert except for a few white Australian pearls, which fluoresce faintly, cultured saltwater pearls--moderately strong to very weak greenish yellow depending on nacre thickness, freshwater pearls--moderate to strong yellowish white.

X-radiograph: Cultured pearls usually show a clear separation between core and nacre, and their core normally looks lighter than the nacre coating. A mantle tissue nucleus will look like a very dark, irregularly shaped void. Natural pearls show a more or less concentric structure, and they tend to look the same tone throughout or get darker in the center.

Bibliography

Books

Ahrens, Joan & Malloy, Ruth. *Hong Kong Gems & Jewelry*. Hong Kong: Delta Dragon, 1986.

Anderson, B. W. *Gem Testing*. Verplanck, NY: Emerson Books, 1985.

Arem, Joel. *Gems & Jewelry*. New York: Bantam, 1986.

Australian Gem Industry Assn. *Australian Opals & Gemstones*. Sydney: Australian Gem Industry Assn, 1987.

Avery, James. *The Right Jewelry for You*. Austin, Texas: Eakin Press, 1988.

Ball, Sydney H. *Roman Book on Precious Stones*. Los Angeles: G.I.A., 1950.

Bauer, Jaroslav & Bouska, Vladimir. *Pierres Precieuses et Pierres Fines*. Paris: Bordas, 1985.

Bauer, Dr. Max. *Precious Stones*. Rutland, Vermont & Tokyo: Charles E. Tuttle, 1969.

Bingham, Anne. *Buying Jewelry*. New York: McGraw Hill, 1989.

Blakemore, Kenneth. *The Retail Jeweller's Guide*. London: Butterworths, 1988.

Bruton, Eric, *Legendary Gems or Gems that Made History*. Radnor, PA: Chilton 1986.

Ciprani, Curzio & Borelli, Alessandro. *Simon & Schuster's Guide to Gems and Precious Stones*. New York: Simon and Schuster, 1986.

Dickenson, Joan Younger. *The Book of Pearls.* New York: Crown Publisher's, 1968.

Farn, Alexander E. *Pearls: Natural, Cultured and Imitation.* London: Butterworths, 1986.

Farrington, Oliver Cummings. *Gems and Gem Minerals.* Chicago: A. W. Mumford, 1903.

Federman, David & Hammid, Tino. *Consumer Guide to Colored Gemstones.* Shawnee Mission, KS: Modern Jeweler, 1989.

Field, Leslie. *The Queen's Jewels.* New York: Abrams, 1987.

Fisher, P. J. *The Science of Gems.* New York: Charles Scribner's Sons, 1966.

Freeman, Michael. *Light.* New York: Amphoto, 1988.

Gemological Institute of America. *Gem Reference Guide.* Santa Monica, CA: GIA, 1988.

Gemological Institute of America. *The GIA Jeweler's Manual.* Santa Monica, CA: GIA, 1989.

Gemological Institute of America. *Proceedings of the International Gemological Symposium 1991.* Santa Monica, CA: GIA, 1992.

Goldemberg, Rose Leiman. *All About Jewelry.* New York: Arbor House, 1983.

Greenbaum, Walter W. *The Gemstone Identifier.* New York: Prentice Hall Press, 1988.

Idaka, Kimiko. *Pearls of the World.* Tokyo: Shinsoshoku Co., 1985.

Jackson, Carole. *Color Me Beautiful.* New York: Ballantine, 1985.

Japan Pearl Exporters' Association. *Cultured Pearls.* Japan Pearl Exporters' Association.

Jewelers of America. *The Gemstone Enhancement Manual.* New York: Jewelers of America, 1990.

King, Dawn. *Did Your Jeweler Tell You?* Oasis, Nevada: King Enterprises, 1990.

Kunz, George Frederick. *The Curious Lore of Precious Stones.* New York: Bell, 1989.

Kunz, George & Stephenson, Charles. *The Book of the Pearl.* New York: Century Co., 1908.

Liddicoat, Richard T. *Handbook of Gem Identification.* Santa Monica, CA: GIA, 1981.

Lintilhac, Jean-Paul. *Black Pearls of Tahiti.* Papeete, Tahiti: Royal Tahitian Pearl Book, 1985.

Bibliography

MacFall, Russell P. *Gem Hunter's Guide.* New York: Thomas Y. Crowell, 1963

Matlins, Antoinette L. & Bonanno, A. *Jewelry & Gems the Buying Guide.* South Woodstock, VT: Gemstone Press, 1987.

Marcum, David. *Fine Gems and Jewelry.* Homewood, IL: Dow Jones-Irwin, 1986.

Miguel, Jorge. *Jewelry, How to Create Your Image.* Dallas: Taylor Publishing, 1986.

Miller, Anna M. *Gems and Jewelry Appraising.* New York: Van Nostrand Reinhold Company, 1988.

Muller, Andy. *Pearls.* Kobe: Golay Buchel Japan, 1990.

Nadelhoffer, Hans. *Cartier Jewels Extraordinary.* New York: Harry Abrams, 1984.

Nassau, Kurt. Gemstone Enhancement. London: Butterworths, 1984.

O'Donoghue, Michael. *Identifying Man-made Gems.* London: N.A.G. Press, 1983.

Preston, William S. *Guides for the Jewelry Industry.* New York: Jewelers Vigilance Committee, Inc., 1986.

Rosenthal, Leonard. *The Pearl and I.* New York: Vantage Press, 1955.

Rosenthal, Leonard. *The Pearl Hunter.* New York: Henry Schuman, 1952.

Salomon, Paule. *The Magic of the Black Pearl.* Papeete, Tahiti: Tahiti Perles, 1986.

Schumann, Walter. *Gemstones of the World.* New York: Sterling, 1977.

Shirai, Shohei. *Pearls.* Okinawa, Marine Planning Co. Ltd., 1981.

Smith, G.F. Herbert. *Gemstones.* London: Pitman, 1949.

Taburiaux, Jean. *Pearls: Their origin, treatment & identification.* Radnor, PA: Chilton, 1985.

Webster, Robert. *Gemmologists' Compendium.* New York: Van Nostrand Reinhold, 1979.

Webster, Robert. *Gems.* London: Butterworths, 1983.

Webster, Robert. *Practical Gemmology.* Ipswich, Suffolk: N. A. G. Press, 1976.

Zucker, Benjamin. *Gems & Jewels.* New York: Thames & Hudson, 1984.

Articles

Austin, Gordon T. "Tennessee is the Pearl of U.S. Gem Production." *Colored Stone.* May/June, pp. 29-30, 1991.

Austin, Richard. "Pearls and the Jewelry Maker." *Gems and Minerals.* January, pp. 46-48. 1980.

Berrenblatt, Alena Joy. "Everything Plus Pearls." *National Jeweler.* October 16, pp. 32-44, 1991.

Brown, Grahame. "The Genesis of a Pearl--An unlikely fairy-tale." *Wahrongai News.* December, 1990.

Crowningshield, Robert. "Cultured Pearl, Accidentally Tissue-Nucleated. *Gems & Gemology.* Fall p. 175, 1991.

Crowningshield, Robert. "Green-dyed Natural Pearls." *Gems & Gemology.* Fall p. 175, 1991.

Crowningshield, Robert. "Remarkable Cultured Pearl." *Gems & Gemology.* Fall p. 176, 1991.

Crowningshield, Robert. "Two different Mabe Pearls." *Gems & Gemology.* Fall p. 177, 1991.

Crowningshield, Robert. "Rare Assembled Cultured Blister Pearls." *Gems & Gemology.* Summer p. 111, 1991.

Crowningshield, Robert. "Pearls: from Baja California." *Gems & Gemology.* Spring, p. 42, 1991.

Crowningshield, Robert. "Dyed Black Cultured, Origin of Color." *Gems & Gemology.* Winter, pp. 296-7, 1990.

Crowningshield, Robert. "Uncommon Cultured." *Gems & Gemology.* Winter, p. 297, 1990.

Crowningshield, Robert. "Gray Baroque Cultured." *Gems & Gemology.* Fall, p. 224, 1990.

Crowningshield, Robert. "Well-Worked Pearl." *Gems & Gemology.* Summer, pp. 155-6, 1990.

Crowningshield, Robert. "Irradiated." *Gems & Gemology.* Winter, p. 244, 1988.

Crowningshield, Robert. "Pear-shaped, Saltwater." *Gems & Gemology.* Winter, p. 245, 1988.

Crowningshield, Robert. "Imitation." *Gems & Gemology.* Summer, p. 114, 1988.

Crowningshield, Robert. "A Rare Cultured Pearl." *Gems & Gemology.* Summer, p. 114-5, 1988.

Crowningshield, Robert. "Early 'Japanese Pearls'." *Gems & Gemology.* Spring, p. 49-50, 1988.

Crowningshield, Robert. "Eroded Natural Pearls." *Gems & Gemology.* Winter, pp. 238-9, 1986.

Crowningshield, Robert. "Pearls with Unusual Drilling Features." *Gems & Gemology.* Spring, pp. 50-51, 1986.

Crowningshield, Robert. "Imitation Pearls." *Gems & Gemology.* Summer, p. 111-2, 1985.

Crowningshield, Robert. "Pearl Simulants, Shell Hinges." *Gems & Gemology.* Spring, p. 45, 1985.

Crowningshield, Robert. "Dyed Cultured Pearls." *Gems & Gemology.* Spring, p. 229, 1984.

Crowningshield, Robert. "Accidental, or "Keshi," Pearls?." *Gems & Gemology.* Fall, pp. 169-170, 1984.

Crowningshield, Robert. "Cultured Pearl Mystery." *Gems & Gemology.* Fall, p. 170, 1984.

Crowningshield, Robert. "Imitation 'Rice Grain' Biwa Cultured Pearls." *Gems & Gemology.* Fall, p. 170, 1984.

Crowningshield, Robert. "More Imitation Pearls." *Gems & Gemology.* Fall, p. 170-171, 1984.

DelRe, Nicholas. "Natural- and Treated-Color Black Cultured Pearls in the Same Necklace. *Gems & Gemology.* Fall, p. 175, 1991.

DelRe, Nicholas. "A 'Teething' Problem." *Gems & Gemology.* Fall, pp. 175-76, 1991.

Depasque, Lorraine. "Prime Time for Pearls." *Modern Jeweler.*" November, pp. 44-60, 1988.

DiNoto, Andrea. "No wonder the ancients believed that pearls grow in the brains of dragons." *Connoisseur,* August, pp. 76-87, 1983.

Dirlam, Dona, Misiorowski, Elise & Thomas, Sally. "Pearl Fashion Through the Ages." *Gems & Gemology,* Summer, pp. 63-78, 1985.

Edelstein, Cindy. "Opposites Attract." *Jewelers' Circular Keystone.* October, pp. 77-100, 1990.

Edelstein, Cindy. "Pearl Classics are Back." *Jewelers' Circular Keystone.* April, pp. 53-57, 1990.

Edelstein, Cindy. "Pearls: The Must Accent for '89." *Jewelers' Circular Keystone.* April, pp. 44-64, 1989.

Edelstein, Cindy. "Pearls: Ride the Fashion Wave." *Jewelers' Circular Keystone.* October, pp. 34-58, 1988.

Federman, David. "The ABC's of Pearl Beauty." *Modern Jeweler.* September, 1989.

Federman, David. "Exotic Pearls, The New Fancy for Fancies." *Modern Jeweler.* September, pp. 43-47, 1991.

Federman, David. "Biotechnology: A New Dawn for Pearl Farming." *Modern Jeweler.* September, pp. 40-48, 1990.

Fritsch, Emmanuel & Misiorowski, Elise. "The History and Gemology of Queen Conch 'Pearls'." *Gems & Gemology.* Winter, 208-221, 1987.

Fryer, C. W. "First American Freshwater Cultured Pearls from Tennessee." *Gems & Gemology.* Winter, pp. 229-30, 1984.

Gemmological Association of Great Britain. "Defining the Thickness of Nacre on Cultured Pearls." *Gem and Jewelry News*. December, p. 7, 1991.

George, C. Denis. "The Black Pearls: History & Development." *Lapidary Journal*, April, 136-147, 1971.

Goebel, Marisa & Dirlam, Dona. "Polynesian Black Pearls." *Gems & Gemology.* Fall, p. 130, 1989.

Hanano, June, Wildman, M. & Yurkiewicz, P. "Majorica Imitation Pearls." *Gems & Gemology.* Fall, pp. 178-88, 1990.

Hargett, David. "Gray Cultured Pearls." *Gems & Gemology.* Spring, p. 97, 1990.

Hargett, David. "Chipped." *Gems & Gemology.* Fall, pp. 173-4, 1989.

Hargett, David. "Pinked." *Gems & Gemology.* Fall, p. 174, 1989.

Hargett, David. "Black Cultured Pearls." *Gems & Gemology.* Fall, p. 166, 1987.

Hargett, David. "A Cultured Pearl Puzzle." *Gems & Gemology.* Summer, p. 104, 1987.

Hiss, Deborah. "Pearl: The Organic Jewel." *Jewelers Circular Keystone."* October, pp. 61-65, 1988.

Hurwit, Karin. "Treated' Mabe Pearls." *Gems & Gemology.* Fall, p. 177, 1991.

Hurwit, Karin. "Cultured 'Demi-Pearl'." *Gems & Gemology.* Summer, pp. 110-11, 1991.

Hurwit, Karin. "Cultured Calcareous Concretions." *Gems & Gemology*. Summer, p. 153, 1990.

Hurwit, Karin. "Pearls: Cultured with Colored Bead Nuclei." *Gems & Gemology*. Fall, pp. 222-223, 1990.

Hurwit, Karin. "Cultured Pearl, Treated Black." *Gems & Gemology*. Winter, p. 240, 1989.

Hurwit, Karin. "Demi-pearl." *Gems & Gemology*. Fall, p. 174, 1989.

Hurwit, Karin. "A 'Fossilized Pearl' from Utah." *Gems & Gemology*. Fall, p. 174, 1989.

Hurwit, Karin. "Natural Pearl & Diamond Tiara." *Gems & Gemology*. Spring, p. 50, 1988.

Hurwit, Karin. "Cultured Black Pearl." *Gems & Gemology*. Winter, pp. 234-5, 1987.

Hurwit, Karin. "Pearls: An unusual clam 'pearl'." *Gems & Gemology*. Spring, pp. 45 & 46, 1987.

Hurwit, Karin. "Imitation Pearls, 'Coque de Pearl'." *Gems & Gemology*. Winter, p. 239, 1986.

Hurwit, Karin. "Freshwater Cultured Pearls from China." *Gems & Gemology*. Summer, p. 111, 1985.

Hurwit, Karin. "Abalone Pearl." *Gems & Gemology*. Fall, p. 169, 1984.

Hurwit, Karin. "Dyed Cultured Pearls." *Gems & Gemology*. Winter, p. 229, 1984.

Kane, Robert. "Freshwater Natural." *Gems & Gemology*. Fall, pp. 223-224, 1990.

Kane, Robert. "South Seas Cultured Pearl." *Gems & Gemology*. Fall, pp. 172, 1988.

Kane, Robert. "Damaged Mabe." *Gems & Gemology*. Spring, p. 45, 1985.

Kane, Robert. "Natural Seed Pearls and Glass Imitations." *Gems & Gemology*. Fall, p. 171, 1984.

Koivula, John and Kammerling, R. "Pearls: Two remarkable natural freshwater pearls from Texas." *Gems & Gemology*. Summer p. 115, 1989.

Montgomery, George E. "Pearls--/gems from the sea." *Gems and Minerals*. January, p. 79-80, 1980.

Moses, Thomas. "Freshwater 'Rosebud' Pearls." *Gems & Gemology*. Summer, p. 111, 1991.

Moses, Thomas. "Assembled Pearl." *Gems & Gemology*. Winter, p. 240, 1989.

Porter, Bruce. "The Black Pearl Connection." *Connoisseur."* April, pp. 120-126, 1991.

Reilley, Barbara. "American Pearls: Prospects & Problems." *Jewelers' Circular Keystone."* August, 95-102, 1990.

Reilley, Barbara. "Pearl Sales: Lustrous Outlook for the '90s." *Jewelers' Circular Keystone."* April, 58-62, 1990.

Schupak, Hedda. "Pearl the Versatile Jewel." *Jewelers' Circular Keystone.* October, pp. 84-96, 1991.

Schuster, William. "US Cultured Pearls." *Jewelers' Circular Keystone."* January, pp.182-186, 1988.

Smith, Jane Victoria. ""Pearl Jewelry: New Demand for Quality." *Jewelers' Circular Keystone."* October, pp. 59-70, 1987.

Sweaney, James & Latendresse, John R. "Freshwater Pearls of North America." *Gems & Gemology.* Fall, pp. 125-45. 1984.

Walowitz, Hedda. "Treasures from the Deep Sea." *Jewelers' Circular Keystone.* October, pp. 86-88, 1988

Ward, Fred. "The Pearl." *National Geographic."* August, pp.193-222, 1985.

Welch, Clayton. "Pearls and Their Apparent Colors." *Gems & Gemology.* Spring, p. 46, 1987.

Weldon, Robert. "Pearls." *Jewelers' Circular Keystone.* September, Part II, p.174, 1991.

Periodicals

Colored Stone. Devon, PA: *Lapidary Journal* Inc.

GAA Market Monitor Precious Gem Appraisal/Buying Guide. Pittsburgh, PA: GAA.

Gems and Gemology. Santa Monica, CA: Gemological Institute of America.

The Guide. Chicago: Gemworld International, Inc.

Lapidary Journal. Devon, PA: Lapidary Journal Inc.

Jewelers Circular Keystone. Radnor, PA: Chilton Publishing Co.

Modern Jeweler. Lincolnshire, IL: Vance Publishing Inc.

National Jeweler. New York: Gralla Publications.

Palmieri's Auction/FMV Monitor. Pittsburgh, PA: GAA

Rock & Gem. Ventura, CA: Miller Magazines, Inc.

Miscellaneous: Courses, Leaflets, etc.

"Cultured Pearls." The American Gem Society.

Gemological Institute of America Gem Identification Course.

Gemological Institute of America Colored Stones Course. 1980 & 1989 editions.

Gemological Institute of America Pearls Course.

"Grading and Information Guide." Midwest Gem Lab.

"Hints to select your cultured pearls." Rio Pearl.

"I am a pearl." Mastoloni Pearls.

"Mastering Cultured Pearls." Adachi America Corporation."

"Pearl: Miracle of the Sea." American Gem Society.

"Pearls of Japan." Japan Pearl Exporters' Association."

"Perle Noire: Quality comes first." Tahiti perles S C.

"Quality Cultured Pearls Price List." Adachi America.

"A Selling Guide for Retailers." Japan Pearl Exporters' Association.

"A Shopper's Guide to Cultured Pearls." J. C. Penney.

"Treasures from the Sea." Shogun Cultured Pearls.

"What you should know about cultured pearls." Jewelers' of America.

Index

Order Form

To: International Jewelry Publications
P.O. Box 13384
Los Angeles, CA 90013-0384 USA

Please send me:

___ copies of **THE PEARL BUYING GUIDE**

Within California $20.51 each (includes sales tax)   _____

All other destinations $18.95 US each   _____

___ copies of **THE DIAMOND RING BUYING GUIDE.**

Within California $14.02 each (includes sales tax)   _____

All other destinations $12.95 US each   _____

___ copies of **THE RUBY & SAPPHIRE BUYING GUIDE.**

Within California $21.60 each (includes sales tax)   _____

All other destinations $19.95 US each   _____

Postage & Handling for Books

USA: first book $1.50, each additional copy $.75   _____
Canada & foreign - surface mail: first book $2.50, ea. addl. $1.50   _____
Canada & Mexico - airmail: first book $3.75, ea. addl. $2.50   _____
All other foreign destinations - airmail: first book $9.00, ea. addl. $5.00   _____

___ copies of **DIAMONDS: FASCINATING FACTS.**

Within California $4.28 each (includes sales tax)   _____

All other destinations $3.95 US each   _____

Postage for Diamonds: Fascinating Facts
USA: $0.55 per booklet   _____
Canada & Mexico - airmail: $0.80 per booklet   _____
All other foreign destinations - airmail: $1.25 per booklet   _____

Total Amount Enclosed   _____
(USA funds drawn on a USA bank)

Ship to:

Name_____

Address_____

City_____ State or Province_____

Postal or Zip Code_____ Country _____

Order Form

To: International Jewelry Publications
P.O. Box 13384
Los Angeles, CA 90013-0384 USA

Please send me:

____ copies of **THE PEARL BUYING GUIDE**

Within California $20.51 each (includes sales tax)   _____

All other destinations $18.95 US each   _____

____ copies of **THE DIAMOND RING BUYING GUIDE.**

Within California $14.02 each (includes sales tax)   _____

All other destinations $12.95 US each   _____

____ copies of **THE RUBY & SAPPHIRE BUYING GUIDE.**

Within California $21.60 each (includes sales tax)   _____

All other destinations $19.95 US each   _____

Postage & Handling for Books

USA: first book $1.50, each additional copy $.75   _____
Canada & foreign - surface mail: first book $2.50, ea. addl. $1.50   _____
Canada & Mexico - airmail: first book $3.75, ea. addl. $2.50   _____
All other foreign destinations - airmail: first book $9.00, ea. addl. $5.00   _____

____ copies of **DIAMONDS: FASCINATING FACTS.**

Within California $4.28 each (includes sales tax)   _____

All other destinations $3.95 US each   _____

Postage for Diamonds: Fascinating Facts
USA: $0.55 per booklet   _____
Canada & Mexico - airmail: $0.80 per booklet   _____
All other foreign destinations - airmail: $1.25 per booklet   _____

Total Amount Enclosed   _____
(USA funds drawn on a USA bank)

Ship to:

Name_____

Address_____

City_____ State or Province_____

Postal or Zip Code_____ Country _____

OTHER PUBLICATIONS BY RENEE NEWMAN

The Ruby & Sapphire Buying Guide: How to Spot Value & Avoid Ripoffs

A guide to buying, evaluating, identifying, and caring for rubies and sapphires.

Discover:

- How to choose a good-quality stone
- How to tell a fake from a real ruby or sapphire
- How to compare prices and save money
- How to buy gems abroad

"**Solid, informative and comprehensive** . . . dissects each aspect of ruby and sapphire value in detail and quizzes the reader on key points at the end of each chapter. . . a wealth of grading information . . . *The Ruby & Sapphire Buying Guide* is a definite thumbs-up for both the unskilled and semiskilled buyer and seller. There is something here for everyone."
C. R. Beesley, President, American Gemological Laboratories, New York. *Jewelers' Circular Keystone*

"**Highly recommended** . . . includes a great deal of gemmological as well as commercial information; text photographs are clear and cover many situations for appraisal which have rarely been put forward in gemmology texts before. . . . useful to the gemmology student as well as to the dealer or purchaser of jewelry."
The Journal of Gemmology, a publication of the Gemmological Association of Great Britain

"**Well-written**--not so technical that you would need a dictionary to understand what is written and, most important, the information in it is all pertinent to anyone who wants to buy and sell colored gemstones. I have recommended this book to all my students and I enthusiastically recommend it to anyone interested in colored gemstones. Well done!"
H. B. Leith, teacher-gemologist, master goldsmith

204 pages, 10 color and 86 black/white photos, 7" by 9", $19.95 US.

AVAILABLE AT bookstores, jewelry supply stores, through the Jeweler's Book Club, the GIA or by mail: See reverse side for order form.

Diamonds: Fascinating Facts

An informative booklet with entertaining facts, poems, and statistics about diamonds.

A novel and appropriate greeting card to include with a diamond gift. It comes with a 6" x 9" white envelope. The inside front cover is designed to allow for a personal message.

Full-color, 16-page, self-cover booklet with six 5" x 7 1/2" photos, $3.95 US.

The Diamond Ring Buying Guide:
How to Spot Value & Avoid Ripoffs

A comprehensive guide to evaluating, selecting, pricing, and caring for diamond jewelry.

Discover:

♦ How to judge diamond quality and jewelry craftsmanship
♦ How to detect diamond and gold imitations
♦ How to choose between platinum, white gold, and yellow gold
♦ How to select a ring style that's both practical and flattering
♦ How to compare the prices of diamonds and jewelry mountings

"Filled with useful information, drawings, pictures, and short quizzes. . . presents helpful suggestions on detecting diamond imitations, in addition to well-though-out discussions of diamond cutting, and how the various factors can influence value . . . a very readable way for the first-time diamond buyer to get acquainted with the often intimidating subject of purchasing a diamond."
   Stephen C. Hofer, President, Colored Diamond Laboratory Services, *Jewelers' Circular Keystone*

"Will definitely help consumers . . . Written in a popular style with lots of personalized examples, the book should be easy reading for the young people who are thinking about their first diamond purchases."
   Lapidary Journal

"A wealth of information . . . delves into the intricacies of shape, carat weight, color, clarity, setting style, and cut--happily avoiding all industry jargon and keeping explanations streamlined enough so even the first-time diamond buyer can confidently choose a gem."
   American Library Association's *Booklist*

"A fact-filled text devoid of a lot of technical mumbo-jumbo. Sellers . . . might do themselves a favor by making this book available to those clients who are eager to find that optimum blend of value, quality and service. This is a definite thumbs up!"
   C. R. Beesley, President, American Gemological Laboratories, New York.
Jewelers' Circular Keystone

"Highly informative . . . *The Diamond Ring Buying Guide* is a useful book for the first-time diamond buyer, the gemologist, who needs a good review on diamonds, and the retailer seeking more information to give to customers."
   GIA's Gems and Gemology

AVAILABLE AT bookstores, jewelry supply stores, through the *Lapidary Journal* & Jeweler's Book Clubs, the GIA or by mail: See reverse side for order form.

151 pages, 85 black and white photos, 7" by 9", $12.95 US.

Order Form

To: International Jewelry Publications
P.O. Box 13384
Los Angeles, CA 90013-0384 USA

Please send me:

___ copies of **THE PEARL BUYING GUIDE**

Within California $20.51 each (includes sales tax)   _____

All other destinations $18.95 US each   _____

___ copies of **THE DIAMOND RING BUYING GUIDE.**

Within California $14.02 each (includes sales tax)   _____

All other destinations $12.95 US each   _____

___ copies of **THE RUBY & SAPPHIRE BUYING GUIDE.**

Within California $21.60 each (includes sales tax)   _____

All other destinations $19.95 US each   _____

Postage & Handling for Books

USA: first book $1.50, each additional copy $.75   _____
Canada & foreign - surface mail: first book $2.50, ea. addl. $1.50   _____
Canada & Mexico - airmail: first book $3.75, ea. addl. $2.50   _____
All other foreign destinations - airmail: first book $9.00, ea. addl. $5.00   _____

___ copies of **DIAMONDS: FASCINATING FACTS.**

Within California $4.28 each (includes sales tax)   _____

All other destinations $3.95 US each   _____

Postage for Diamonds: Fascinating Facts
USA: $0.55 per booklet   _____
Canada & Mexico - airmail: $0.80 per booklet   _____
All other foreign destinations - airmail: $1.25 per booklet   _____

Total Amount Enclosed   _____
(USA funds drawn on a USA bank)

Ship to:

Name_____

Address_____

City_____   State or Province_____

Postal or Zip Code_____   Country _____